I Love You All My]

by Shari Berens

"I Love You All My Life"

Letters from World War II
Compiled by Shari Lynn Ward Berens, granddaughter of William and Ann Genzer

"I Love You All My Life"

Letters from World War II
Compiled by Shari Lynn Ward Berens, granddaughter of William and Ann Genzer

The compilation you are about to read are letters written primarily by my maternal grandmother, Sarah Ann Quattlebaum Genzer, to her husband, William Adolf Genzer, after he was drafted into the United States Army during World War II. They were married on April 12, 1940, so at the time they are nearing their fourth wedding anniversary. Baby Ann, as she was always called, is 23 years old at the time of the first letters in Spring of 1944, and Bill is 27. Their first child, Carol Ann, (my mother), is about 18 months old at the time of the first letters. Eventually, Bill and Ann will spend 72 years in marriage together before Ann passed away in June 2012, just shy of her 92nd birthday.

There are also letters that Bill received from his parents, William and Matilda Genzer, known as Willie and Tillie; Tillie's parents, George and Julia Brandt; his sister, Lorraine, knows as Sis or Lorry; and from a few other relatives or friends periodically. Those are included here as well to add context. The majority of these letters, of course, are from Bill's wife, Ann, who wrote to him almost every single day that they were apart.

One thing I found interesting about these letters is how personal and intimate they are, as well as how funny it is that Ann writes as if she were dictating to someone. Her personality comes through loud and clear – so funny at times, a little bit nagging at other times, but always loving and devoted. At times, I could actually hear her saying these things as I read them!

Historically, these letters provide an interesting look at family life during the latter part of World War II.

Regarding the format of this book, the first dates listed are from the postmark on the envelope. Then, any other dates or days are from the letter as written. Any text in italics is Shari's comments regarding the content in that letter, or details about family or friends mentioned.

Enjoy!

Shari Berens

October 2014

Me as a baby with my grandmother, Sarah Ann (Baby Ann) Quattlebaum Genzer, circa 1966

William Adolf Genzer, (born November 9, 1916), c. late 1930's

Sarah Ann Quattlebaum Genzer, (born July 13, 1920 in Lafayette, Louisiana), c. 1938-1939

March 12, 1944 – from Ann Genzer, 1203 Missouri Ave., Houston, TX
To: Pvt. William A. Genzer
38671305 Co. C
Ft. Sam Houston
Reception Center
San Antonio, TX

Theo and Bobbie Frank are mentioned in the letter below. Bobbie is Ann's older sister, Effie Roberta Quattlebaum Frank, and Theo is Bobbie's husband. At the time, Bobbie is 25 years old and Theo is 28.
The "squirt" and the "chicken" refer to Bill and Ann's daughter, Carol Ann, who is 18 months old at this time.
Aunt Tennie refers to Ann's father's older sister, Tennie Agnes Quattlebaum Bergeron, 62 years old.
"Mama" refers to Ann's mother, Sarah Ann Mouton Quattlebaum, who is 52 at the time.

Tuesday

Hi Sweet,

Golly, the dear old man who brings news of loved ones just dropped a letter from mine in the little black box on the front porch. You can never say that you're not unusual – a letter written all over the page, whether upside-down or sideways, you get the job done alright! You still didn't mention anything about your cold. I really developed a dill. I woke up with a sore throat and rubbed my chest right away and started talking cold capsules, so I guess I've got it by the tail. I didn't think they'd give you shots with a bad cold. Please don't forget to mention this.

And don't ever say Uncle Sam isn't there on the job either. In the same mail, I received our initial payment of $80.00. I almost fainted – you know I've heard so many stories of how long it took before the allotment started coming. My March payment, so they inform me, will arrive about the first of April. That's OK by me!

Honey, did you pay up your insurance? I believe I have here the latest receipts, and what about your checks from I.B.M.? Will they mail them here or must I pick them up at the office? Your S.O. checks, I mean. I imagine Frankie will call me, though. You picked some S.O. checks up at the office Thursday, were they all you had coming?

I keep thinking of a thousand things I should have gotten straight that Thursday instead of being so selfish.

The chicken has just gone to bed for her nap. That's why I'm starting this in the middle of the day! Mama and I just finished lunch and she's on the telephone.

Speaking of the telephone – I called Lila Lee this morning and Raleigh got a 6 month deferment. They're thrilled to death about it. I sure hope Van gets his. Theo is pretty sure he's going – did I tell you about the horse? Well, they are keeping Marion and Harper Avis' horse for them and it surprised

6

Bobbie to pieces to learn that Theo could really ride. The kids love "Trixie" and aren't a bit afraid of her. She's very gentle and even Bobbie wants to ride her.

The squirt was calling me. I had to go in and lay her down. She's been so good and other than missing you terribly we're both doing all the good. Mama's on her way to the store. We've been taking turns about doing different chores and in general everything is working out fine.

I'm going to quit now so I can get myself cleaned up for the afternoon. (I sure do miss our shower!) We'll write more after the queen is abed for the p.m. Bye now...

Sweet! It's five o'clock and guess what I've been doing – The baby and I slept til 4:00! Yes, I was the gal who was going to go clean up about 2:30, wasn't I? She (Carol) didn't go to sleep until almost 1:30, I guess that's why she slept so long. She'll never want to go to bed tonight. Right after I finished page 4, the telephone rang and it was Peggy. She wanted me to answer some questions so I can start getting my allowance from the company. She also wanted your serial number and your sweater size. They sent rather will send, some sort of plaque to me and your mother. Don't tell her because I want it to be a surprise to her. Peggy also said that they were going to send me a service flag and she also said you had picked up all your back S.O. checks. She said your paycheck was there too and she was mailing it to me.

Well, sweet, I guess I'd better go now and get a few things done.

I did – and from the time of the last paragraph, I've fed the baby and she has your letter in a paper bag playing with it.

I really must go now. Aunt Tennie and Mama are beginning to kid me about writing all the time, but see if I care! Ha! I'll write more tomorrow and maybe I'll be able to tell you how much money you made the past few weeks.

Call me again soon, in the meantime, I love you all my life – Bye now.

Ever yours,

Mommy

March 13, 1944 – from 1203 Missouri Ave., Houston, TX; To: Ft. Sam Houston Reception Center, San Antonio, TX

Sunday night

Hello Sweetheart,

Golly, it was swell hearing your voice this morning – rather <u>almost</u> hearing you! I was so surprised that I guess you wondered what was the matter with me. I wanted to ask you so many questions and I couldn't think of a <u>one</u>! One thing – how is your cold, sweet? I was so worried about it. I was also going to ask you if they had started giving you your shots. I wondered, too, if they would give you them with that cold. I hope it's alright by now. The baby's cold is almost gone and I believe we have her cough under control now. I just put her to bed. She was so tired. This house is so big and she has explored every nook and cranny. Sweet little doll, she's waked up every morning calling you. This morning she almost cried.

But I've been a good soldier and after I had my first cry out I've been alright. I know what you must have felt and it made me so ashamed of my actions that it snapped it right out.

 You know I was going to write you Jimmy and Dorothy Powell's address in S.A. (San Antonio) but I'm afraid I'm a little late! Dorothy called me Friday night and they've been doing the same as we. Moving – he's leaving this Friday night. He got the Navy and, not that this has anything to do with the Navy, but she's going to have another baby in August. Jim Jr., is three months older than Carol but she's thrilled to death with it.

We've been busy as cats on a tin roof. We've got everything just about straight now. Just a few more things to do in our room and then I'm going to start sewing. Maybe in three weeks you will be able to get a weekend pass and we can see you. I want you to be proud of me when you see me and our chicken. Speaking of the chick, I asked today if the pictures were ready but they weren't so I guess it'll be Tuesday before they're ready. However, I'd hate to send them before you have a more permanent address because you may not get them. I told you this morning I had a letter from Max. I'm enclosing it. Be sure and write him. His address is:
Pvt. A. M. Groves
ASN 18118697
TNS. GRP. 301
Sheppard Field, Texas

And while I'm on addresses, I'd better send the rest right now. I'm going to print them because that way you won't have to wonder what it is – so here they are:

Lt. Robert W. Collins
01312126 "W" Co.
2nd B. N., 119 Inf. A.P.O. 30
Camp Atterbury

Miss Ore Nell Brandt
Rt. 3, Box 209
La Grange, Texas

Cpl. H.L. Hillin, Jr
38160402
37th Q. M. Pack Troop
A.P.O. 303
Camp Roberts, Calif.

Mr. & Mrs. Grover E. Mouton (Aunt Odette)
(also Daddy's Address)

302 3rd Street
Lafayette, LA.

Mrs. Benton W. Maboules
Rayne, Louisiana

Mrs. T.W. Ratcliffe
338 ½ 15th Ave. N.E.
St. Petersburg, Florida

Mrs. & Mrs. L.H. Van Amburghe
(I'll have to look this up)

If there are any others, be sure to let me know. My eyes are beginning to close on me. I've been taking time out to listen to some programs on the radio. Do you mind? Anyway, speaking of radio – have you been listening to "I Love a Mystery"? I haven't but will start again tomorrow night. I'll write a long letter tomorrow, sweet, to make up for this. I hope you get this, though.

Well, sweet, I'll write more next p.m. so will close now. Be sweet and remember I love you forever – and all my life, too! Bye now.

Love you loads,

Baby Anne

P.S.: On second thought I'll wait until I find out if you get this before I send Max's letter. I love you.

March 16, 1944 – from 1203 Missouri Ave., Houston, TX; To Ft. Sam Houston Reception Center, San Antonio, TX

March 15, 1944
Wednesday

Dearest Pops,

Gosh, I'm sure glad that date above doesn't mean anything more to me than just one more day close to you. All I've heard on the radio today is "Pay your income tax today!" – Thanks babe!

Now, don't start laughing at me when I tell you this, but the dear old battery pooped out on me and I had to ask Mac Douglass to push me until I could get it started. Luckily I had it out of the garage down to the bridge and he pulled me out with a rope. It started pretty quick, though. I guess it's because it's not used to so much leisure.

I guess you've already looked at the snapshots but anyway I'll tell you I've enclosed them. Hope you like them. I'm going to try to get more film. If you can get 1-16, 6-20 film, get it and I'll find the camera. The baby just handed me the card you sent and said "Da-Da" – I told her just once that the card was from you and that was day-before-yesterday! Please get some pictures made. I'm dying to see you in your uniform. I want to have a small one to put in my billfold.

I took the keys over to Mr. Meineke and almost cried when I saw the house. Diapers out on the line, and blue bonnets all in bloom. It made me almost sick. But the thing that made me mad was – the garage doors were open! I almost went over and closed them. You raised me differently!

The chick is walking around in here as big as you please. She can open doors now and believe me, she really has us jumping! Aunt Tennie just came home and she nearly had a fit. Aunt Tennie brought her a little bucket and spade yesterday and she was tickled pink. I guess you can look at the pictures now and see everything I tell you.

I just put the pot to bed for the night and thought I'd dash down a few words. We're sitting in the sun room and Mama is reading and Aunt Tennie is sewing. She is covering our bed lamp and it is just beautiful. She can really sew. She's going on her vacation next week. Just taking a week and I hope we can get down to Newgulf for a day or two. I know both Mother and Aunt Tennie would enjoy it. Aunt Tennie brought a little cart driven by Donald Duck to the baby this evening. She's helping her to get past five o'clock – looking for her Daddy.

I heard "I Love a Mystery" last night and it's really getting good. They're prisoner of Lloyd and April Krieger in an isolated castle on an isolated island somewhere in Africa. The doctor they're looking for is imprisoned in the same castle but they don't know where. Jack was handcuffed to a chair and Doc and Lloyd are playing poker to find out how many hours they have left. It is really good. If you don't get to hear it, I'll keep you informed of the happenings.

Honey, I guess I'd better close now, so I won't get too boring with my silly chit-chat, so until tomorrow, my sweet, be good and keep loving me and our little chicken.

I love you all my life,

Mommy

P.S.: If you're wondering who "Janie" is and where Blatt (a Cpl, I believe) comes in, well, she called me tonight and told me she wrote him frequently and he told her you and he were in the same outfit, or something and that's how it happened. She's the gal Sarah usually runs around with and by the way Sarah has a little girl. Both are fine. Must go now so – bye now – Love You Forever

---

March 17, 1944 – from 1203 Missouri Ave., Houston, TX; To: Sam Houston Reception Center, San Antonio, TX

Susan is Bobbie's second daughter, Susan Elise Frank (later Herrmann), who is 2 ½ years old. "Weese" refers to Louise, who is a housekeeper and nanny that had been with the Robert and Sarah Ann Quattlebaum family for several years.

"Sis" refers to Bill's younger sister, Lorraine Mae Genzer (later Koenig), who is 17 years old.

Thursday

Hiya Honey!

Hope fine. That cold of yours is still worrying me. I had one but it's just about over now. I'm going to rub my throat tonight again though – oops, ran out of ink!

Got the battery back today and it cost me the whole sum of one dollar and fifty cents! Nearly killed me – however the boy over at Romeo's (George) said he would take care of the car for me. I'm going to have him wash and grease it for me soon. He told me whenever I needed service to come early in the morning and he could take more care of it because he's usually so busy in the afternoon. He seems to be a pretty nice boy – don't get jealous. He's the same color as my spots.

Bobbie and Lily just left. They came for B's laundry. Susan has a cold and so has Lily and Jerry and Bruce. Mama has a dill and so does Aunt Tennie. You should see us. Handkerchiefs over our noses for protection to the mess pot.

It's been hot as Hades. We nearly burned down today. It's a little cooler tonight but I hope the sun shines again tomorrow because the ground will be dry and I can let the baby out. She fussed and

Baby Ann's mother, Sarah Ann Mouton Quattlebaum, known by family as Daid (or Dade), and later as Momo by her grandchildren and great-grandchildren, with her three granddaughters - Susan Elise Frank, 2 1/2; Carol Ann Genzer, 18 months, and Robert Dianne Frank, 4.

fumed all day wanting to go outside. She would go to the back door and call "Weese, Weese,..." and once she got mad cause Louise wouldn't answer her and yelled "O- Lo-weese!" Mama and I almost collapsed!

Got a letter from Sis today. Everybody's fine and said that Ralph said you made a very handsome soldier and I'm dying to see you. (More so now.)

Gosh, honey, I just happened to remember you told me not to send anything important because you may not get it. I went ahead and sent the pictures, but thought if you didn't get them , I could always send more shots, and if you did get them, it would do more good than anything I could say.

Your paycheck came today. $92.18 – pretty good, eh? Listen, honey. I'm pretty tired so if you don't mind, I'm going to turn the body in. The squirt seems to think she should get up when Aunt Tennie does and 6:00 rolls around pretty quick – Hope she sleeps later in the morning.

By the way, Jean called me and talked. It was swell of her and, honey, Norma's here. She got in at 9:00am this morning and I haven't gotten to see her yet, but we talked awhile and from what I could get without asking too many questions – Lonnie is shipping out.

Nuff news for Thursday. More Friday – by now, sweet –

I Love You

Mommy

March 18, 1944 – from 1203 Missouri Ave., Houston, TX

To: Pvt. William A. Genzer
38671305
Co. C. Brks. #4
Ft. Sam Houston, TX

Friday

Hello Sweet,

Just received your second letter and I am informed that you haven't received any from me. I started writing Friday night and each night thereafter a letter has been written. It made me feel kinda blue, but then I thought maybe you'd get a whole bunch at a time. Read them in succession – this is the 7th letter I have written, I hope you get them all.
The baby's well but I feel like hell, thank you. I have a cold but imagine just as soon as the flu caps started their job, I'll be skipping rope outside. Another hot day – and I've told you so much in those other letters that you'll have to write and tell me what days you missed hearing from me and I'll try to remember what happened – well – Pat has a boy and Pauline has a girl and Louise Partin is going to

Oklahoma to join Charles. He's being shipped out. And Norma's back – same reason. I sent the snapshots so if you don't get them in a day or two I'll send more. We also got a letter from Max. His address is:
Pvt. A. M. Groves
ASN 18118697
TNO. GRP 301
Sheppard Field, Texas

I sent all the boys addresses so if you haven't received them I will send them again too.

I'll send Max's letter just as soon as I'm sure you're getting my letters.

I'm so glad Ralph went to see you – and while I'm thinking of it – please, I've been begging in every letter for a snapshot of you in your uniform. If you could have a portrait – about an 8 x 10 for my bureau and a little one for the billfold Sis gave you. I hope you get these letters cause if you don't, I'll have to get a typewriter to write that novel you want. If you got Thursday's (last night's), you'll know about your checks – and mine! Yes, I've already received my allotment – 80 bucks and I got it Monday! Then your paychecks (for the first two weeks in March) arrived yesterday. We're doing all the good, eh?

Just found out my fountain pen would write and since it's easier to write with ink than pencil, I'll see what I can do.

I found the bank deposit envelopes and statement but (don't laugh!), I can't make it balance. The bank says we have more money than I do, but I suppose I'll find I failed to enter a deposit.

Well, sweet, I believe I'm going to call it a day. Hope you received the pictures, but if you didn't (I knew I was taking a chance), I can send the negatives back for reprints.

The blue bonnets are in bloom at 1713, and it made me terrifically lonesome, but I haven't cried since the afternoon you left (Proud of me?)

I must write the folks now I'm sending the other set of snapshots – then when I hear from you about whether you received them or not, I can have more made for both of us.

Write as often as you can, sweet, and don't forget a picture for your two girls.

I love you all my life –

Mommy

The Genzer family at the beach, c. 1941 -
Lorraine Mae; Matilda "Tillie"; William "Willie"; and Bill.

Baby Ann and "Sis"

March 19, 1944– from Lorraine Genzer, Newgulf, TX

This letter is from Bill's younger sister, Lorraine Mae Genzer (later Koenig), who is 17 years old. "Mom" and "Pop" are Bill's parents, William Genzer, 47, and Mathilda Julia Wilhelmina Brandt Genzer, 45, at the time. They were called Willie and Tillie by friends and family. "Grandma" refers to Willie's mother (Bill's paternal grandmother), Agnes Knapik Genzer, who is 75 years old. (Willie's father Joseph died in 1925 at the age of 58.) We know that when Lorraine (Sis) mentions "Grandma", she is referring to Agnes because Tillie's parents (George Friedrich Brandt and Julia Hickel Brandt) were called Opa and Oma and are both still living at this time, aged 72 and 69 respectively.

March 18, 1944

Dear Bill,

How's my soldier brother today? It's raining cats and dogs and everything else outside. It poured all night and it looks like it's going to pour all day. It has rained almost every day this week. We tried to have a track meet in school Wednesday and we no more than got started and it began to rain buckets.

We had the meet yesterday, Friday, but the track was still a little damp. That didn't stop Boling though, we came out the winner, Bay City second, and Wharton third and last. Not bad, eh?

How do you like the army life about now? You've had a week to find out a little about it. We saw Ralph last weekend and he said you looked swell in your uniform but naturally I knew you would because you're my big brother. How did you come out on your tests? Ralph told us you were taking a bunch of them and that the outcome would tell whether you would go to O.C. S. or not. I hope the outcome qualifies you to say, "O.C.S. here I come." I'm betting on you.

Ralph also told us that you had missed first call for K.O. Are you still missing it or have you already been stared in the face by thousands of potato eyes? What's this you said in your letter about being a "runner"? You seem to be doing alright. You look up the guys to do the work while you sit tight. Nice work, if you can get it, and you seem to have it.

By the way, have you gotten your hair cut yet? If you have, I'll bet you're a pretty picture. Nice long hair, every bit of a half inch long, I know. You shouldn't worry though: there was a guy at the U.S.O. last week who had all of his shaved off. And, oh boy!, did he look cute! Ugh!!

We had a little hard luck in the neighborhood Wednesday. Mr. Pavlosky, the man who lived in the house set way back from the road to the right of us, died. If you remember him you will know he had a large family. Eleven children, to be exact. One has already graduated and is working for the Phenix dairy in Bay City. One girl will graduate this year and the rest are still rather small. Their youngest are twins, seven months old. It was really a shock to all of us. He had an ulcerated stomach and the ulcers burst. He was operated and part of his intestine was removed but it didn't help.

Mom and Pop, in fact, all of us, are just fine and all are feeling just grand. No one is sick, not even a cold. Mom got rid of that terrible chest cold she had. Mom was terribly worried about that cold you had when you left. Did you have it long? Grandma is fine, too. By the way, have you written her? If you get time, write to her and mention the colatches. It would just tickle her pink. She'd be so proud

to know you enjoyed them. She said that just as soon as you're stationed where you can get packages she wanted to bake some more for you.

Mailman's due – paper's gone – I'll write again – you write soon –

Love,

Sis

March 19, 1944 – from Tillie Genzer, at Box 142, Newgulf, TX – To: San Antonio, TX

This letter is from Bill's mother, Tillie Genzer (Mathilda Julia Wilhelmina Brandt Genzer) who is 45 years old at this time.

Thur, 16th

Dear Bill,

How are you this pretty day. We are all well, hope you are the same.
Got a card from Ann yesterday and gave us your address but said you may be changed anytime, so hope you will get this yet. Well Ralph didn't get married last Sat. I was thinking he just was saying

that to be saying something.

We saw him last Sun and he said you really look good in your new suit. The telegram we send you Mon. Ralph gave us that address. I guess you got it. Let us hear from you often.

We got your card Tue. and was really glad to get it, I will save all cards and letter you write, so I can read them over and over. Excuse this paper. I must get some when I got to Wharton. Our neighbor Mr. Povolskey was operated last week and yesterday he died. He will be buried tomorrow in Wharton.

Grandma and I will go to the funeral.

Well I will close for now.

Be good and write often.

Love from,

Mom, Pop, and Sis

Sat. 18th

Well here is another day gone by. We got your letter and sure was glad to hear from you. And hoping to hear from you often. We will write just as often as we can.

We went to that funeral I wrote Thur you about, it sure was a big one. They had 3 priests for him and a long mass. Last night we went to see Mrs. Povolsky and children. There are 11 children. She is really going to have a time with all those children. It is really raining now and is dark. The lights are out, I am writing by candlelight, it is about 12:30 noon. I hope I can catch the mail mail so I can mail this. I am going to write Ann and Carol a letter too.

Let us know when we can come to see you. We will get Ann and Carol and come over on some early Sun morn. Did you write Grandpa already I know they really would like it.

I must stop now. Be good and Love from us all.

March 19, 1944 – from 1203 Missouri Ave, Houston, TX, to Fort Sam Houston, TX

Saturday

Hi Sweetheart,

Just received your Blatt letter and I suppose you know by now I knew all about it. Gosh it makes me feel swell to know you have a good friend. Golly, if you ever raved about me to anyone as you raved about Jim, I'd be scrumptously happy!
I'm glad you're in the mail room that way you can be sure of receiving your mail. I don't suppose you

have any idea what's going to happen to you, do you? I hope, if you have to go far away at any time, it'll be just for basic.

I just wrote Sis – received a letter from her Wednesday and hadn't had a chance to answer it. Our colds are just about over now, so maybe I can start sewing and doing the things I have to. The baby is fine, but runs around so much she get tired early so rises early. This morning she woke up at 5:30 and Aunt Tennie brought her a bottle and so we both slept til about 8:30. I really needed that extra sleep too.

It's been raining all day and looks as though we're in for more. If this weather would only clear up we might get over these colds.

Aunt Tennie forgot to take your last night's letter with her this morning and I mailed it this afternoon. You'll probably get these two pretty close together. She goes on her vacation Monday so guess I'll have to mail them myself. It might delay a few hours but I doubt very much.

I just went downstairs and called to the paper boy for a chronicle – kinda made me homesick. I hope Jim's taking care of you.

Susan is still coughing but has no fever now, so I guess we're all on the mend. Hope your cold is alright. How many shots have you taken? Which reminds me, I have to have the chicken vaccinated next week (or earlier).

I'm enclosing Max's letter. Hope by this time you've received our snapshots. I know you'll be proud of them. I am. I need one of my soldier boy now to make my gallery complete – please!

Writing every day makes Annie a dull boy, so will end this boresome tale so you can get on with something better. Will try to make fascinating history tomorrow as I can tell you something interesting. So bye now – write soon and remember both your girls love you and ...

Miss you,

Mommy

March 20, 1944 – from 1203 Missouri Ave, Houston, TX, to Ft. Sam Houston, TX

Sunday

Good evening, your nibs??,

No, I didn't do it – I mean I didn't make astounding history today, but your daughter almost did. Yesterday morning, I told you, Aunt Tennie gave her a bottle when she woke up at 5 – well, this morning she decided that worked well one morning, why not try it again? So, the little chicken woke and called "hot-hot" and I just picked her up and brought her downstairs and gave her breakfast.

She ate a half a bowl of oatmeal and was ready to turn in again and slept til 9:30! Can you imagine that? The mess! I hope she doesn't try that again – I'd much rather get up at 7:30 or 8:00 (imagine!) and keep her on her schedule. She's so much better that way.

It turned cold today about 10:00am and the fires started. I sweated like a nigger at election. Mama's been swell about it though and she's even got ventilation in all rooms! A window aopen in this house is history so I guess I haven't fallen down on my h-making project today!

We haven't done a darn thing all day. It's been so nasty I've been afraid to get out with my cold. However if it's pretty tomorrow, I'm going to go to Sears with Aunt Tennie and get the baby out. She's so restless and looks for you constantly.

Bobbie was over today and Theo had ants so they went home early because he wanted to ride his horse!

We're listening to Fred Allen and old Falstaff was just on and I had to take a few moments to listen. They're a bunch of dopes. One of his poems were:
She made an awful fuss
When he kissed her on top of the bus (bust)!
Wasn't that awful!

I'm going over to see Mrs. K tomorrow and want to get over to Mrs. Norris' too. Hope its pretty 'cause Mama won't let me budge if it isn't.

Tell Jim hello for me and that I like him very much just from your description and also ask him if he went to Milby and if he was a Lt. in the R.O.T.C. there. Jean seems to think she knows him. At least she knew a Jim Blatt there. I believe it was Milby – but ask him anyway. I haven't talked to Janie since I wrote last but I want to see Sarah tomorrow night and Janie said she wanted to go with me so we can get it all straightened out then.

I must go now, sweet. It's cold and I'll miss my little (?) bed stove so be good and write soon and often.

Love to you from both your girls

March 21, 1944 – from Ann, 1203 Missouri, Houston, to Ft. Sam Houston

When Ann refers to Mama, she is talking of her mother, Sarah Ann Mouton Quattlebaum. When referring to Mom, she is talking about Bill's mother, Tillie Genzer (Mathilda Julia Wilhelmina Brandt Genzer).

Monday's letter - Written Tuesday morning

Hi, my sweet!

Well, I really had one whale of a time yesterday. About 1:00p.m. had to go to bed with fever 102 2/5 degrees – fine stuff, eh? Well, I've been doing it every day starting Friday so Mama put me to bed and called the doctor (Dr. Hartgraves). She said she didn't know what it was, gave me some cough medicine and told me to stay in bed. As usual, the fever left around 5:00pm. Isn't that funny? The Dr. seems to think its fatigue and strain with my cold. My colds just about gone but I cough so darn hard. The cough medicine was really good last night, tho, it helped me sleep, thank goodness. The squirt slept all night until somewhere around two or three – crawled over and got in bed with me and slept on until 9 am! Can you imagine! Well, now, that I've got all the bad news off, I'll tell you why I didn't write last night. Janie came over and told a very interesting tale. All about Jim and how, if I could go this weekend, he could get you cut so we could see each other – oh golly, wouldn't that be swell! Of course, it's beyond our powers this weekend, but she said if we waited much longer Jim may be shipped – he must be waiting for his orders – has he said anything – I sure hope he's there for quite a while, not only because I hate to see anyone shipped over the waves, but because he's been such a pal and swell guy to the fella I call mine. Janie described him and I know I'd like him. Just as soon as I'm able to get out, I'm going to do all the things I've been planning to do. I'm so glad the baby's alright that I don't mind my ailments a bit. Aunt Tennie and Louise took her out yesterday in the warm sunshine and I guess she'll get to go out again today. The weather looks like it might continue to be pretty – I hope so.

I think I may get out some things to sew as long as I can't get up – I'll go crazy not doing anything. Poor Louise sprained her back and can't stoop or pick anything up. She has a plaster on her back and it's better today. It looks like we're all getting OK now. If I'm free of fever all day, the M.D. says I'll be OK, so here's hoping. The funny thing about the whole thing is – I don't feel bad at all – in fact I feel just grand – so I guess it's just reaction. She said she has several ward wives on her patient list whose husbands have just gone and, just like me, she's sure it's just reaction and just as soon as they rest a few days, they're just as good as new. She also said that's the reason so many boys enter the hospital when they're first inducted – with colds or fever – it's just the readjustment process that the mind and body can't help. Funny, isn't it?

Yesterday was Aunt Tennie's birthday and we had company all day. It helped a lot to get my mind settled so I guess I'm mending.

Gosh, I've done nothing but talk about myself – Forgive me, sweet – but I just wanted you to know all the facts so you could see there was nothing to worry about.

I received a letter from Mom yesterday and they said they were ready for a trip to S.A. (*San Antonio*) anytime I could get ready, so who knows, we may be kicking together come Saturday – oh well, if we don't, I sure wish you'd call me again. Thrill of Thrills! Hearing your beautiful voice!

The squirt's walking all around this morning – helping Mama straighten up. She picks up everything and gives it to Mama and says Da-Da! Sweet mess! She's been so good. Janie had a fit over her, thought she was beautiful and when I showed her the pictures she grabbed one and kept it. I've got to have more made right away. By the way, pops, where's that picture of my favorite soldier boy? I have to have it, so please retaliate!

Gotta go now – running out of stuff and nonsense – so be sweet and call if you can – please.

Loads of love from,

Your two little girls

March 22, 1944 – from Ann, 1203 Missouri, Houston, to Ft. Sam Houston, TX

Aunt Mabel refers to Bob Quattlebaum's younger sister, Mabel Quattlebaum, 50 years old. Grandmother Quattlebaum is Bob's mother, Katherine Bell Harris Tuttle Quattlebaum who passed away 10 years before in 1934.
Ann's parents, Robert Dudley Quattlebaum and Sarah Ann Mouton Quattlebaum, are 56 and 52 years old respectively at the time.
Aunt Odette is Ann's mother's younger brother Grover's wife, Marie Odette Burguterres Mouton, 48 years old. Grover and Odette's so , Grover Ernest Mouton II, served in World War II and was a Japanese prisoner of war during the Bataan Death March in April 1942. He was eventually released and lived to be one month shy of 100 years old.
I believe Emile and Jean are also Mouton cousins, but am unsure of exact relation.

Tuesday p.m.

Hello again sweet –

How's the G.I. Joe? Thought I'd start your letter now and maybe get in a few words before they come upstairs. I just finished dinner. I like being sick this way. I feel just grand but Mama wants me to stay in bed for a couple days just to be sure. I had fried chicken on toast, homemade vegetable soup and lemon pie (Aunt Mabel baked it for Aunt Tennie's birthday) and I haven't tasted pie crust like that since Grandmother Quattlebaum died – she really used to make pies – but for goodness sakes – don't tell Louise!

Since I've been an invalid I haven't been able to listen to "I Love a Mystery". Have you heard it? If so, I wish you'd give me a short synopsis of it. The poker game was the last I heard of it.

Aunt Tennie just came up for the tray and I told her I was going to go over to Aunt Mabel's and take lessons on pie crust. Then maybe you'll like civilian life again, huh? How about that.

The baby is playing with a bunch of spoons at the bottom of the stairs and calls up to me and we carry on a conversation. The folks can't get over it. She's getting so everything is sounding like something. The other morning she said, "Mama, I wanna go home" – Did I tell you? Seems as I did.

Mama just brought Carol up. She's getting so big. Try's to do everything. She shut the door and said, "There!" – She's hollering "Through!" from the bathroom now. Mama just put her on the johnny.

Well, just put the squirt to bed so now I'll finish telling you about "My Day".

First, Dorothy called. I couldn't talk to her but Mama did and she said that Van is going. He was accepted by the Navy but I don't know when he leaves. Then Jean called and said she received a letter from Aunt Odette and she said Emile is leaving Monday.

Then I got a surprise. Max called. Well, I went to the phone – had to. He was at the station and had been waiting on a cab 40 min! I asked him if he could come out but he said his train was leaving at 7 (and this was about 2:30 or 3:00pm), so I told him I thought it was silly, his having to wait on taxis that way and told him to come on out and get the car. He didn't want to but I insisted so he said he'd

Left: Baby Ann's paternal grandmother, Katherine Bell Harris Tuttle Quattlebaum. Her father's family, the Tuttles, had lived in America since 1635.

Below: The Quattlebaum Family, 1917, at their home on Kane Street in Houston. Standing from left: Tennie Agnes Quattlebaum and her husband Perl John Bergeron, (Judge) Samuel Mercer Quattlebaum and his wife Katherine, Sarah Ann "Daid" Mouton Quattlebaum. Kneeling are: Nell Louise Quattlebaum, Hazel Juanita Quattlebaum, and Baby Ann's father Robert Dudley "Bob" Quattlebaum.

come. He was on his way to the Valley, probably his last furlough before being shipped. Anyway, he never showed up, nor did he call. I thought it was funny but Mama said he probably ran into someone who insisted on taking him around and he just didn't have a chance to call. He'll probably write soon and tell me how sorry he is about it. Poor kid, I did want him to come out so we could do something for him. Did you receive his letter? I want you to be sure and write to him.

Well, I guess I've told you just about everything that's happened today.

Oh yes, I've fixed all the financial matters. I stopped the bond deduction the day Peggy called. She said she'd find out if there was a surplus, and if so, she'd have them send it. The checks are O.K. so you can rest your little head.

Listen, this has been worrying us to pieces. You said Buddy Gardner was shipped to Camp Fannin – now, where in Sam Hill is Camp Fannin. Would appreciate enlightenment immediately!

This has been going on long enough now so will draw to a close now – no not yet. The judge who fined me 10 bucks has been drafted. I can't remember his name, but I hope you're his top kick someday (yum, yum!)

Now I gotta go! Be sweet and write soon. Chick and I miss you and I love you.

The old lady

P.S.: Well, sweet , I guess I'll have to write more – Max just came. He said he waited until 5:00 for the cab and that Frankie and Grover and Ethel went to the Ritz for dinner, then Ethel and Frankie went somewhere and Grover brought Max here. He was here only a little while but I'm so glad he could come. He isn't being sent over, just being transferred – to Denver and he's going to be a bomb-sight engineer – can you imagine! I'll tell you more about what he said in my tomorrow night's dispatch. Seems when I take the pen in hand I say "My baby isn't going to get a long letter tomorrow" and lo and behold, before I know it, here I am on page seven! I'm getting writer's cramp now so really must go – bye now.

Love to you,

Mommy

March 23, 1944 – from Ann, 1203 Missouri, Houston to Ft. Sam Houston, TX

Wednesday

Hello Honey,

Just finished eating so decided to start my letter to you. I've been awfully popular since you left. Max wanted to take me to dinner at the Ritz last night and Ralph called tonight wanting to take me to a show! How'm I doing, eh? He has a job with the American National Life Ins. Co., and as a salesman, too! He told me how swell you look in your uniform so now, sure 'nuff, I can't wait for the pictures. Hope they're better than you seem to think! Did you get a G.I. haircut? You haven't told me a thing about how you're living or anything about Army life – I guess you're waiting to tell me that when I see you. Maybe I'll be up tomorrow and get out in the afternoon. Hope so. Then maybe we can start planning a trip. Do you think you'll be there long or do you know?

The baby's fine – she's playing right here by the bed with your billfold. I have some of my things in it and she takes it all out and puts it back in. The sweet little doll. She was walking around here this afternoon with one of Mama's goofy hats on – had a veil on it, too. She was precious! She just saw your pictures in the billfold and she got real stiff and pointed to it saying "Da-Da". So thrilled – it really thrilled me and then she kissed it and nearly died laughing. Sweetest thing I've ever witnessed!

I guess I got the idea you weren't receiving my letters from you. You skunk, you told me that you'd "been there a whole week and hadn't received a single letter!" – so what do I surmise? Keerect! Now, explanation please.

This has been a dull day so I guess I'll close now. Be sweet and it's really swell hearing from you so often. You don't have to write every day, sweet, I understand. I mean it, too.

We'll try to see you soon. Call when you can and let me know how I can call you. I might want to some dark night – so let me know.

I love you always,

Mommy

March 23, 1944 – from Tillie Genzer, Newgulf, TX

This letter is from Bill's parents, Tillie Genzer, 45 years old, and William Genzer (Willie), 47 years old. There are several spelling and grammar errors, some of which I corrected.

Dearest Son,

How is everything by now, hope you are still in the same place. Do it rain in San Antonio like it do here and in Houston. We really had a hard rain yesterday again, it rains so often everyday or every other day. Of course today it is pretty again. I don't know how about tomorrow.

We didn't get to plant our potatoes yet and don't know when we will. I was in Wharton yesterday to get some feed and car lisons. They sure are small – they are square 2x2 in. I told Pop he better be careful, when he is going to put them on, so he won't loose them while he is putting on.

Sis had a letter from Ann saying they may come over to see us with Mrs. Tennie while she is on her vacation. But didn't know for sure yet. Did you see any one you know yet? You know Emma Amman, she is there at one of those camps working. I thought she may be at the one you are, she is working in the kitchen, that is where I think Martha told me she is working but I don't know at what camp.

Well I think I must stop now and get this mailed.

Write as often as you can.

Lots of love from us all,

Mom, Pop, and Sis

March 23, 1944 – from George Brandt, La Grange, TX, to Ft Sam Houston, TX

This letter is from Bill's maternal grandparents, George Friedrich Brandt, 72, and Julia Hickel Brandt, 69. There are several spelling errors, as the Brandts' native language was German, so I corrected some of the spelling.
Ore Nell Brandt is Bill's cousin, 19 years old at the time. Ore Nell is Tillie's younger brother George Henry Brandt's daughter.

Dear Bill,

Your letter received and sure glad to hear from you. Ore Nell and I were talking together about you yesterday at the mailbox. My Bill do not write. He is there now about two weeks. I am going to write to Ann and find out so we get the address so we can mail to you. Now we are satisfied. I give Ore Nell your address so she can write you too. It is nothing how here since you left it is raining her all a time. We have not planted any corn yet it is too wet. I hear from San Antonio every day at 7 o'clock AM over K.T.S.A. so if you have a special, you can send it over K.T.S.A.
That be all for today. Hope to hear from you some.

Love,

Your Grandparents
(George and Julia Brandt)

March 24, 1944 – from Missouri Ave, TX, to Ft Sam Houston, TX

Thursday

Hello, my darling, hello,

And how's the guy today? Hope the cough is better. Mine seems to be just about gone today. Thank goodness I'm out of that bed, anyway.

I was a little disappointed when you didn't enclose the pictures in your letter but after I saw those 10

George Friedrich Brandt, (1872-1960), and his wife Julia Hickel Brandt, (1875-1955). George emigrated to America from Langwarden, Oldenburg, Germany when he was 14 years old to join his older brother, Emil, as they looked for land in Texas for their family to live.

<u>pages</u> I almost fainted with delight!

My mama didn't raise no foolish chilluns! I did just what you suggested for the checking acct. I wrote my last check day before yesterday for cash and I believe it'll hold me over until after the first of April. I wanted to do that so I could start keeping up with it as I write checks and keep to the $80.00. I had to deposit your March 15th check in the checking acct because I had kept it long enough. I couldn't get to town myself so I thought it best to just go ahead and mail it in. And the more our balance is the less they charge for the checks I'll write.

Honey, I may be pretty clever at certain things, but that S.O. stub and overtime business has me down. Absolutely! I'm trusting to the company. Peggy will probably be over next week and I can get her to check it but as for me – Greek!

Thinking of Cpl. Rudy Baker, I guess she was happy to hear he was a "permanent party". Hope WAG has that luck. It'll be swell when we can be together again.

You haven't mentioned Cpl. Blatt lately. He hasn't been shipped, has he? And that reminds me. Janie said that if I wanted to go up for a weekend, Jim could get rooms at the... - gosh, some hotel anyway. Ask him and if he can we'll let you know when we'll be up and you can make reservations – At the St. Anthony, I believe, she said. Ralph said he'd drive me up Sat afternoon and come back Sunday night. I've had so many offers that it's almost too much – if I come breezing up, don't be surprised. If I took the baby, I'd have to be sure of reservations but if I came alone it wouldn't make too much difference where we stayed. This is so much pipe-dream though – probably won't get to see you until Easter. We'll be there with bells on then, you may be sure.

Well, here is it 8:20 – the chicken bathed, bottled and put to bed.

Just before I went upstairs for the above tasks Jean called. She said Max called her last night before leaving and said he sounded too gay – kind put-on. Joe's idea of the whole thing was that he was so tired and also so taxed by his first visit here since Mardelle passed away that he must have been under a terrific strain. Poor boy. She's feeling fine and wants me over just as soon as I can get a chance. I hope to this next week. She also said the office was thrilled to hear from you.

Well, I guess I'd better go now so be sweet and hope that we will be seeing you very soon. I love you all my life and miss you terribly.

Kisses,

Mommy

P.S.: Will send coat hangers tomorrow – how many do you want. I'm sending 6 or 8 – Will that be enough?

Love you, Me

March 24, 1944 – from Ore Nell, Rt. 3 Box 209, La Grange, TX, to Ft Sam Houston, TX

This letter is from Bill's younger cousin, Ore Nell Brandt (later Frerichs), 19 years old.
When she mentions Opa, she is referring to their grandfather, George Friedrich Brandt, 72, who moved to America from Germany and was the first generation of Brandts in America. Oma is his wife, Julia Hickel Brandt, who is 69 years old at the time.

Dear Bill,

Don't be surprised that you're hearing from me before you wrote me but I happened to be at the mail box when Opa received your letter. He had just asked me the day before if I had heard anything from you or Lawrence and I just had to say "no". He was really tickled to hear from you and furnished me with a pencil so I could copy your little address.

I wrote Winnifred and Lawrence yesterday and here's hoping I get an answer soon. When Ralph came home, we just automatically stopped hearing from them. Good ole Ralph Gus.

I've been disappointed so far I haven't heard from Ann. Yet since you all were here, I would have written her but really don't know where to write her. Guess you've been getting all the letters she's writing I don't blame her. You're very lucky too to have such a sweet wife and Baby. We too are very fond of them!

I guess one of these days you'll be hearing from Opa. He and Oma are just fine and so are the rest of us here. We're puttering along as usual. Still raining though so Daddy or anyone else here on the place hasn't even planted a seed of corn much less cotton. The sun is shining now – let's hope it stays that way.

Say Bill, you really have been lucky getting into mail work. Hope you get to stay in S.A. (*San Antonio*) a while yet.

Let us hear from you soon again and let us know if you're moved.

Love to you from all of us,

Ore Nell

March 25, 1944 – from 1203 Missouri, Houston, to Fort Sam Houston

Tuesday

Hi Sweet,

I believe this is going to be another one of those letters written by the hour. One paragraph now – 2 or three later and a few added tonight to close. It's now about 10:30am and the mess is walking around me. I'm going to take Dorothy to the M.D. today for her 6 weeks check-up. It looks like rain again but it looked just like this yesterday morning. Then about 3:00, the sun came out and you would have sworn it was mid-July! So hot!

I suppose you're still in S.A. Hope so anyway, because I'm really looking forward to seeing you – whether in S.A. or H. Janie wrote Jim last night – she wants to go up there so no telling what she told him. Remember, if it's at all possible, I'd rather you came here – It would be so much easier. But don't forget to call Thursday night! I talked to Ralph this morning. He hasn't bought a car yet and asked if we wanted to sell Yuhudi – Wot say? Anyway, he gets off Sat at 11:00am, so we'd get away from here not until after 12 – or maybe one o'clock. Then we'd leave Sunday night, so if you can't come and want me to, we can make arrangements Thursday nite. Of course you probably won't know Thurs night and if you can't find out by then whether or not you can get a pass then you can call me Friday nite. I'm going ahead and mailing this now – rather the postman will pick it up about 1 – that way, you'll get it Wed – if I wait and give it to Aunt Tennie, you won't get it until Thursday and it would be too late to let me know when you're going to phone. Write just as soon as you get this so I can know right away when you are planning on calling.

Well, sweet, I'm going to draw this to a close. I'm going in now to put the baby's potato on, so had better go. Do you really want me to come up? I wasn't sure when you left because you didn't act very enthused about the thought. I won't feel hurt, be sure and let me know.

I love you,

Baby

March 25, 1944 – from 1203 Missouri, Houston

Friday

Dearest,

It was so swell hearing your voice again. However at times I got to thinking that you weren't just calling from the office saying you'd be home and would I like vanilla or chocolate tonight for a change – then I really felt funny. Then I thought how near you were. Just a few hours drive and it made me want to hop in Yuhudi and see what would happen. No telling what I'd liable to be doing! The chick woke up again this morning calling you and I told her you had called and told her everything you said. She sat still and when I got through, was perfectly content to go on about her own business. She really does miss you.

Peggy just called and said she had a letter from you. She said it was addressed to Leonard so she hadn't opened it, waiting for him to come back. She said Leo or Joe had heard from you and had some news about your being classified an I.B.M. Tabulating Engineer and Don Gamel is coming in Monday so may have further news. I figured the reason you hadn't said anything about it to me was that you didn't want to get my hopes up too much. That's all right, sweet, but you know it'll get to me sooner or later and I'd much rather hear it from you.

The mail man just arrived bearing two (2) letters from my love. I almost fainted. Your letter that was written yesterday and one yesterday morning. Fine stuff! I like that. So you'd like to be out on some creek somewhere – And whom would you like to be with? Consider carefully before answering this one!

I'm glad you're back to work again. And I'm back on my job too. Dr. Hartgraves is the M.D. and yes I know how you feel about female doctors but this one is one of the best and she knows what's the matter with me. I told you what she said and my cough was just a hangover from my cold. Just like yours, that's all. Don't worry, sweet – it makes me worry to think you are.

I've got to go up and dress now. I have to go to the grocery store, so I'm going to close this for now. Maybe I'll have something else to tell you this evening.

I don't know Tennie's address yet but will get it from Norma when I see her. Hope to get by today or tomorrow. She's working, by the way, at Mading's as a cashier. Both Don and Ralph work there, too, so I guess it's alright. Her hours are from 3pm to 10pm.

Here it is 8:10 – just came down from putting the little girl to bed. She's been a love today. Louise came back from the store this evening and Carol went in to greet her. She called out to Louise – "Whatdya buy, Weese?" – we almost dropped dead!

Listen honey, I believe I'm going down and get a suit. Since I hope to become a traveling woman, I think that would be the best thing to get, don't you?

And look, another thing – I want to know – are you definitely classified I.B.M. Maintenance Man and will you do that sort of work anywhere and everywhere or just what branch you belong to and everything. Tell all, pal!

Maybe I'll see you next weekend. Hope, hope, hope!
I'm gonna go now, sweet. I'm going to listen to a couple radio shows and then to bed.

Oh yes – call Leon C. Lampe (Gladys and Leon) and say hello. Also I wish you call Myra Louise (Babe) Antonio and her mother, Cousin Myra. Tell them you're stationed there and everything . I'd sure like it if you would.

Will be waiting for your letter tomorrow – hope you didn't forget the pictures. I can get a 1-16 so get the films. Get any you can. I can always find a camera. Bye now and love you loads –

Miss you,

Mommy

March 28, 1944 – from Missouri Ave, Houston, TX - To Co. C, Brks 4, Ft. Sam Houston, TX

Monday night

Hello sweet,

How's everything? Just put the mess to bed. Finished bathing and undressing her, and here it is 8:00 already. I'm getting ready to go over to Sarah's now. Janie's coming by for me. I talked to her this evening and she said if I'm planning on going to S.A. (*San Antonio*) this week-end she said she was going to write Jim to stay there. She's coming too – that is, if I go. I told her I wouldn't know until about Thursday and would have to wait until I talk to you. I'll be waiting for you to call Thursday nite – huh? What do you think? Hope Jim can get you home again this week-end – we could have so much fun –

11:30 pm:

Just got home. Sarah's baby is precious! I told Janie the only way we'd go up there would be for Ralph to drive us up. He called tonight but I was already gone – he said he'd call again tomorrow. I'll write then and let you know what's up. I'd rather you come home though, because the chicken is alright now so you'd really enjoy yourself this time. However, I would like to see your "home"! I promise to write a long letter tomorrow so if you'll pardon this one, I'll go on to bed. Good nite, sweet. Sleep tight.

I love you all my life,

Me

Baby Ann and Bill with Baby Ann's older sister, Bobbie, and her daughter Dianne, c. 1941.

March 29, 1944 – from Missouri Ave, Houston, TX

Bobbie, 26, is Ann's older sister Effie Roberta Quattlebaum Frank. Ann mentions Bobbie's two daughters, Dianne, who is 4, and Susan, who is 2 at the time. Theo is Bobbie's husband, who is 28.

Tuesday pm

Hello again!

Just thought I'd sit down and tell you what went on after I finished your letter this morning. I put on the baby's potato and took her outside. All the neighbors came over. Mrs. K brought Tootie over and Betsy and Temple, then Marie and Dolores. We really had a party. Then at 11:45, we came in and I fed Carol then went to get Dorothy (after I put the chick to bed) and took her to the Dr. Mrs. Boggs and Norma were over there and since were in such a hurry we promised Norma we'd stop by the drug store for a drink. We did and stayed until 2:00. Then Janie and I went to town. I finally got my Christmas present and I know you'll adore it. I want to get a snazzy blouse and hat and bag and gloves and shoes to match. I'm spending your hard earned dough, babe, but I'm sure you'll think it's worth it when you see me. Or at least I hope so! I just got the suit today so I know I'll wear it when we come this weekend. Hope I find a pretty blouse. The other accessories can come later. Out of my next allotment! Oh, golly, when you get this you'll probably have a headache wondering how much I paid for the suit. That can wait, my friend!

Haven't done so much in ages! Bobbie and the two kids were here when I got home and Theo came and we ate then went outside and let the little guys play out for awhile. Then they left and we stayed outside until a gust of cold wind came up – everybody on the street was yelling! We all dashed in and wack! Just like that – winter is here again! Fine stuff, eh? I just put the mess to bed and am getting ready to do a little sewing so will close.

Bye, my sweet – don't forget to call –

I love you,

Mommy

March 30, 1944 – from Missouri Ave, to Ft. Sam Houston, TX, but address is crossed out with change to Camp Lee, VA (to be forwarded)

Wednesday

Good afternoon, my sweet,

Just received your letter and I hope you do come here because it would be swell. I really mean it. You'll get to see the mess and we can go somewhere Saturday night without a huge hotel bill – oh boy – that will be swell – don't you think?

I'm going over to the Variety store just as soon as Carol wakes up. I want to get a pattern. You remember that brown crepe I bought just before Christmas? Well, I'm finally going to start sewing on it! If I cut it out tonight I may be able to finish it before the weekend. It doesn't matter though because I have my suit (you'll love it!), and I'm going to dress up for my husband this weekend!

That's swell about Lee's writing you and swell news it was too! I only wish I could tell someone about how perfectly grand those guys have been to you. Of course, you know I won't mention a word of it. I'm scared I'll jinx the whole business even if you didn't mind about talking! You never have to worry about my saying a thing out of turn – not since the $40.00 raise business. (Will I ever live that down?)

I'll quit now so I'll have something to write about tonite. Bye now and am keeping my fingers crossed for that weekend pass – Hope Jim comes with you. I'm dying to meet my poppy's benefactor. If you come will you come the same way? Hope so – gets you here earlier and I like that!!

Thursday

I wrote this yesterday before you called last night as I suppose you know by now. After Carol woke up, I went on over to the Variety Store and couldn't find the pattern I wanted, so I just bought one for a pinafore for Carol and came on home. When I got here, Ralph called and asked what I had planned on doing and I told him nothing so he said he was coming out and was going to take me to a show. Well, right after that you called and I decided to go with him anyway because Bobbie had the overnight bag and I thought Ralph could drive me out. Mama said we weren't even around the corner good when you called back. Then when we got to Bobbie's, I had to wait about 20 min for the telephone and finally had to ask the party line to get off! Then when I got the operator it was fully 5 minutes before she contacted the right operator. I felt better about it after I talked to you, too, sweetheart. It made me feel funny telling you bon voyage that way, but still I think it really would have been better for us that way. If I had come up and not been able to see you but for a few hours and had to go to the hotel by myself (if you were having so early, I'm sure you couldn't possibly have obtained permission to get out all night). I would have been even more disappointed than I was. This way – I'm sure it's best, don't you? I'm so glad I got to talk to you though. If you hadn't known and just shipped, it would have been kinda tough. If you're pretty far from home and can only get a short leave, let me know ahead of time and I'll meet you halfway – or anyway, somewhere so we can be together as much as possible.

Van is leaving April 12 – that's a heck of a date for a separation, isn't it? Emile came through here yesterday morning and is on his way to California. However, he may be headed to Corpus for all we know. I'm just dying to know where you're going – I didn't want to know so that I wouldn't be able to tell a lie when people asked me where you were. You're still in S.A. to my knowledge and will be until I get that anxiously awaited letter. Hope you get to write as often. I'm writing in the dark, so to speak, because I know you'll be reading this after you've reached your destination and possibly after I know where you are.

I guess I'd better quit now so I can give this to the mail man. He's due any moment, so be sweet. I love you all my life. Take care of yourself and remember I'm doing the best I can.

With love,

Baby

March 31, 1944 – from Bill's parents, Willie and Tillie Genzer, Newgulf, TX, again sent to Ft. Sam Houston, and then forwarded to Camp Lee, Virginia.

Grandma refers to Willie's mother and Bill's paternal grandmother, Agnes Knapik Genzer, 75. I am unsure who Julie is, possibly a cousin.

Friday noon

Dearest Son,

Received your letter and was glad to hear from you.

We are glad those Lt. were so nice to you and ask you to come to Houston whenever they go.

We got home 9:30 o'clock, we left right after Ann got back from taking you. Went to take Grandma to Julie's house but they weren't there yet so Grandma stayed at the neighbor's house she know them, but she didn't come back yet. When we were coming home right out of town, we picked up a sailor and when we got to Rosenberg. We picked up 2 soldiers. They all went with us to Wharton. The sailor was going to Corpus (Christi) and the soldiers were going to Victoria.

We are having some nice weather now hope it stay that way for awhile. We sold two tons of dry hay out of the barn and that green hay too, they cut it yesterday. I hope they get it in sat. Jack Chaptman bought it all. We are going to try and get our garden planted next week.

We are going to a school play at Newgulf tonight. The junior class is giving a play. Wednesday night, they had a style show at Boling picture show. Sis styled her suit she made and got first prize, there were about 20 to 25 in the style show all that made the dresses in school. And had some tap dancers too.

Well, I guess I must close for today and get this off.

Love from us all,

Mom, Pop and Sis

April 1, 1944 – from 1203 Missouri, Houston, to Ft. Sam Houston, Forwarded to Camp Lee, VA

Friday
Mar 31, 1944

Hi, you lucky dog!

Just found out where you're going and something about what you're going to do. However, I'm still pretty much in the dark. You know Janie. She finds out everything and I suppose it's alright now anyway to tell your destination to the folks here. I told them this morning. You told me not to say anything until Friday, so I hope that's ok. I didn't tell them what you were going to do, though because I don't know myself.

Daddy came in Wednesday night and he said he was so sorry he missed you. He will probably be here until Sunday. Hope so anyway.

Boehme called last evening said everything was swell with him and Polly. John's had sore throat for a couple days but doesn't seem to be very sick. He said to give you his regards. Talked to Van and he's leaving Apr. 12. I told you that though. Then Ralph came out last night and an enjoyable chat ensued for all. Daddy enjoyed meeting and talking with him so much. He thinks the Ripper boys are alright. They all seem to think you and Ralph have more than just a family resemblance. They say if Ralph's pug nose were like yours you could be twins. I hope Ralph comes out often.

This morning about 7:30, Max came in. We had breakfast together, then he wanted me to go with him but since my mornings are pretty well taken care of, he's coming back after I put Squirt to nap and he's going to take me to lunch.

Friday p.m.

Max took me to the Ritz for lunch and I'm so glad I got the chance to talk to him because he told me quite a few things about himself and how he's finding himself. It's tough but his mother gave him something to think about and he feels more contented than he has since Mardelle died. I'll tell you all about it when I have more time. He's upstairs asleep now. I'm to wake him up about 4:10. His train leaves this evening at 5:00. We're going by the office first, then I'm taking him to the station. Poor kid, he's really tired. Stayed up all night. Hope you get more rest on your journey than he did. Did I ever tell you how much I adore you and just what you mean to me? Then remind me sometime – it might be interesting!

I'm going now, sweet, so – hey – wait, just received a letter from <u>that</u> guy! So glad you wrote – I really didn't expect it. Yes – I know who my lover is, and I'm not likely to forget it. If Jim's anywhere around – tell him I appreciate his sending his love. I hope I get to meet him this weekend. I believe he plans on coming in, isn't he? Well, I really must go, so be sweet and love me forever, for I Love You All My Life.

The Old Lady

April 2, 1944 – from 1203 Missouri, Houston, to Ft. Sam Houston then forwarded to Camp Lee, VA

Saturday

Dearest One,

Tonight I'm alone. Susan has had fever and a sore throat so Mama, Aunt Tennie, and Daddy went out there. The baby has had a cold and slight temperature so I didn't think I ought to take her out there. The measles are everywhere so if Susan is getting them I don't want to expose Carol any more than accidentally. I just put her to bed. Poor little heart, she was so tired and wanted you when she went to bed. She called you. We both miss you terribly. I was hoping you would wire me when you reached camp. Is it Camp Lee in Virginia? You know even Jim could be wrong. Or Janie could have misunderstood him.

Van just called. He said he wanted to write so be sure to write him as soon as possible.

When I took Max to the station, we went by the office to say farewell. Joe was there. Jean was operated on last Sunday. I didn't get a chance to talk to him alone so haven't any other news other than she's getting along fine. I'm going to try to get to the hospital tomorrow. You know she's gained 21 pounds in 6 months. That might be a tuma *(?)* – wouldn't you say?

I'm dying to know about your training. What you're planning and studying for. Joe asked me if I thought the deal at Kelly had fallen through and I told him that from what you had told me over the phone, it sounded like it. I also told him that you told me you were going to write him and Leo just as soon as you knew what the deal was. He seemed pretty tickled. Peggy and Frankie kidded me about picking up another soldier when my boy was still so green. Peggy said I looked so good with my 107 pounds that she was seriously thinking of sending hers to the Army. She got the ha-ha from Leonard, I'll bet. I didn't get to see him or York but I know they're plenty busy!

Well, sweet, I guess I'd better go now. Please excuse the pencil I can't find my pen. I'm going to have to address the envelope with Mama's pen so will end this now. I love you so much it really hurts. I'm sorry we can't be together Easter or on April 12, but even so, we're just one more day nearer each other.

Until tomorrow, my love –

All yours,

Mommy

April 3, 1944 – from Missouri Ave, to Ft. Sam Houston, then forwarded to Camp Lee, VA

Louise is the housekeeper/cook and help in the Quattlebaum household. She is called Weese (pronounced Wee-Zee) by Carol.

Sunday

Hi Sweet,

How's my soldier tonight, my darling? We've been listening to the radio and just finished putting our little mess to doe-doe land – I guess that's how you spell it! I can't find my fountain pen. I'm using Mama's and it's kinda tricky. I think our oldest niece (*Dianne*) had something to do with it. Louise said she saw her with it yesterday. A little grilling is in the offing – eh, wot? (*sp?*) Susan is fine. Just a sore throat, she's free of fever and so is Carol. I gave Carol the cough medicine she used when she had her last cold. Well, it had soured and that's what made her sick. We gave her milk of magnesia and she's alright tonight. Had me buffaloed for awhile there though. Looks like every week – and we have a Saturday party.

Well, my sweet, next week we begin our fifth year together. You know when we married everyone said we looked so cute together – your tallness, my squat low – oh gee, I wish we were looking cute together right now.

I wish I knew whether you'd arrived safely or not. Daddy's still here. Came in Wednesday night and here it is Sunday – oh dear, do you think it means he's been fired? If the censor reads this, I'm only kidding!

I'm getting ready to write your Mom and Pop. This will probably be short because I don't know what to discuss with you. If I only knew what and where and why of your position, I could ask you a few questions. Oh, well, I have hopes the mail man and post office dept may get together with the U. S. Army and let me in on a few of the secrets tomorrow around 1:00pm (1st mail delivery).

We had another one of those freak northers today. I came out of church about a quarter to eleven and the sky was bright. I got to the first red light and the sky was dark – that quickly! By the time I got home the wind was a gale and cold as the d____!! Luckily I had on my suit so was warm and didn't feel it much at all. It had started sprinkling when I got in the house and it rained until after 3:00. It's not very cold now because it's clear. Hope it stays like that.

If I keep this up you'll want me to quit so I'll do so before you do. The baby is ok, and so am I, so there's no need to worry now. I love you and boy!, will I be glad when I can start your way. Be as grand as you always were and remember we both love you and miss you. How about some more pictures.

Love you always,

Mommy

April 4, 1944 – from Missouri Ave, forwarded to Camp Lee, VA

Monday

Hello you skunk,

Remind me to send you the divorce papers tomorrow! Here I was all steamed up today when the envelope with my name in your handwriting was sitting up in that little black box on the front porch. I rushed in, thinking my lover had divulged all! Then the surprise! You so and so. That "thing" was from Palestine and when I got through with it, you ought to be glad you weren't within earshot!

Nuff nonsense for now.

Wish you could have seen our little one just before I put her to be. She had on her little blue dotted seersucker and you know how short it is – well she looked just like a doll. (The bangs have been cut again.) She was pushing her "baby" around in the little pink baby carriage – I almost cried with longing for you at that moment.

We changed the furniture around in my room. The baby's bed is on the right side and I sleep on my old side now (I still can't get used to a whole bed by myself.) Anyway, both the chick and I feel at home more now.

Mama and Aunt Tennie just got back from the hospital. Helen Bond (I mean Shannon) has an 8 pound boy. They say he's beautiful. He's a blond so will probably take after the Quartbottles. Pat, as you remember, looks just like Gilbert.

I tried to get Ralph just now but he wasn't in. Daddy left this morning. Everybody's well. I'm making this short and snappy, sweet, because Betsy just called and we're going to see "Lassie Come Home". They say it's grand. I hope I like it. I'll write tomorrow, sweetheart and remember…

I love you all my life,

Yours,

Mommy

April 5, 1944 – from Missouri Ave, forwarded to Camp Lee, VA

Ann mentions "The Limited" below which is apparently a train, as Ann's father, Robert Dudley "Bob" Quattlebaum was a train engineer. "Dade" refers to Ann's mother, Sarah Ann Mouton Quattlebaum, whose nickname was Dade.

Tuesday
April 4, 1944

Hello sweetheart,

Received your card today and was glad to hear you'd at least reached St. Louis safely. Wish I knew where you are at this moment. I know when you read this you'll be at camp but I mean at – or rather between – 8:30 and 9:00 on the above date. Bob Hope is on. Don't forget to tell me when you answer this.

Daddy came in again tonight. He brought the Limited in. He dead-heads back tomorrow morning. We were really thrilled to see him. I only wish I could have the thrill Mama had.

Sunday's Easter. Can you imagine! I want to take the baby's picture in her Easter outfit. That white dotted swiss that Mary Elizabeth gave her and her white silk coat and a white dotted swiss bonnet

Robert Dudley Quattlebaum, 16 years old, c. 1904.

Bob Quattlebaum, date unknown.

with pink roses on the front – Hope I can get film.

Carol is fine. I'm pretty sure that she just had an upset stomach. So did Susan. Dianne had it today – she had fever up to 102, mouth reading. She's alright tonight, though. Betsy's two kids had it last week, too. The doctors say it's all over town. Mrs. MacPhails' son (lives across the street on the side) had an acute indigestion and almost died last night. I hope ours is over for a time.

I feel swell – it feels so good to feel good you ought to see me. I eat like a horse and am gaining back those four pounds I lost – darn it!

Hope the mail tomorrow brings along letter from my own guy. I want to know so much and I know so little! Please write as soon as you can. I love you all my life and I miss you more every day. So does the baby. Yesterday morning when we were at breakfast, Mama was upstairs and the baby said something that sounded like "Where's Dade", and Daddy said "You want Dade?" She said "Uh uh! I want my Daddy!" I almost cried – I'll be loving you always.

Your sweetheart

Tuesday p.m.

Dearest,

This is the second letter I've written today to you so if it's short it's just because I've already told you all anyway. (There's the most gorgeous piece on the radio – "I'll be seeing you" – I want to see you so bad.)

Honey, I got your letter of Saturday today. You said you were going to start looking for an "apt" Sunday – sweetheart – take <u>anything</u> – a room will do – then we can keep looking for something better together. I doubt whether you'll get any other thing than a room. I do want to tell you though that I want you to <u>wire</u> me as soon as you get the place. It's pretty hard to find seats on the trains and I imagine I'll have to have a 5 to 10 days reservation before I can leave. I've found out that much, so (I can hardly stand this waiting) let me know by a <u>straight</u> telegram.

I'm anxious to be with you so much that I can hardly do anything or say anything that makes sense – so I guess I'd better close. I wanted to tell you so much but I can't think of anything except the part about – wire when you find something – anything – just so we can be together – Please hurry and I promise to be more patient.

I love you all my life –

Good night, sweet

Mommy

P.S.: (Not unless they bite you first)

April 6, 1944 – from 1203 Missouri Ave, Houston – forwarded to Camp Lee, VA

Thursday, April 6, 1944

Dearest one,

This is for last night. Ralph came over and we talked until 11:30 and I was so tired I thought I'd just scribble a note this morning so you wouldn't be disappointed when mail call came and you didn't have a letter from your two squirts.

Ralph has an 18-year endowment plan I believe we should take out for Carol. I'm going to send a copy of the policy so you can see it. It really is a swell thing and I believe the best I've ever heard of.

We're both well. Hope I get a letter today. Am going to the beauty parlor – finally! It's been 6 weeks since the mop has felt water. Don't you think it's about time?

I would love to write a long letter but since this is Wed's letter and I'll write again tonight, I think I could wait to tell you a few things then. Will be seeing you soon I hope and loving you always.

Yours,

Baby

April 7, 1944 – from 1203 Missouri Ave, Houston, forwarded to Camp Lee, VA

Inside the envelope, Ann writes: "I love you always"

Thursday, April 6 - p.m.

Hello again,

No letter again today and I'm kinda getting' the blues – gee, I hope I get a letter tomorrow.

Got a letter from Mom today. She's waiting for the mail man too these days. I've already answered it. I also wrote OreNell and Opa. Since the first of the week, I've had a little time on my hands. Ralph has come out a couple of times. He called and wanted to take me to a show and have lunch with him. He didn't work today – he didn't sleep all night because his eyes hurt him so much. He called me this morning to find out who the best eye specialist here in Houston is. He went to Dr. Gore (the one who operated on Aunt Tennie) and he said his eye-balls are all scratched caused from the scar of the granulated eye-lid operation. I hope your eyes haven't bothered you. He said he felt like he had grains of sand in his eyes. Remember how yours bothered you every once in a while? Anyway, he said he also said he was lacking in Vitamin "A" in his eyes. He is allergic to smoke and the reason it flared up like that – he has to stay in the office on Wednesdays, and it's smoky and foul in there from the cigars and cigarettes of the rest of the salesmen. Have you ever heard of anything like that?

I had my hair washed today. It really looks beautiful. I have a surprise for you but it'll have to wait about a week! Now you'll have a chance to find out how much suspense you can stand! Ha, Ha!

When I went over to the beauty shop today, I talked to Granny. I suppose you know all this by now but, anyway, Doris and Joe are up there at Lee. She has a nice house so (don't say anything yet), but I'm hoping to pay her a little visit if you're thinking of making that your address for a little while.

If you get to Washington D.C., call Aunt Tennie's first cousin – May Quattlebaum – you can find it in the phone book. B.J.'s in Norfolk, or rather near there. I'm going to get his address and write him. Maybe you'll get to see each other.

Must go now, sweet, so even if I do fuss at you about not receiving letters, I love you all my life and miss you terribly –

Baby

April 10, 1944 – from Missouri Ave, to A.S.N. 38671305, 1st Platoon, Co. "O", 7th Q.M.T.R., Camp Lee, VA (1st letter to this address)

Saturday

Hello Honey,

I've written every day but I don't imagine you've received any of my letters yet. I'm sending this Air-Mail because I want you to get it in a hurry. I just received your address – 5 days later! So if you want a letter to reach me within a couple of days you'd better fly it here.

Just in case you don't know it by now, you're in the same place Joe Cobb is. I'm writing Doris just as soon as I finish this. She has a free room house and believe you me, I'm coming to see her sometime!

My letters will tell you all the news so I won't go into that. Please write and tell me what you're training for and just what's expected of you and don't forget to write Jean and Joe. She's still in the hospital. Hope I get to see her soon.

The baby and I are both well and just got back from spending the night with Theo and Bobbie. Theo and Janet came in this morning and Bobbie's going back with them. Everybody's well and so is Mom and Pop. Have you written Opa? Be sure to at once. I wrote yesterday – Ore Nell, Opa, and Pop and Mom.

I must close now – just waiting to hear from you. How about an Air Mail? I love you and we both miss you more each day.

Kisses to "My Bill",

Mommy

April 10, 1944 - from Bill's sister Lorraine Mae Genzer, 17 years old, Newgulf, TX

Dear Bill,

We were all very happy when we received your letter telling us you had finally reached your destination. So you're in Virginia! Well, that's an awful long way off.   One of the first things we did after we got your letter was to get the map and look up Petersburg. It's not very far from the Atlantic coast, is it? I also noticed when looking at the map that it wasn't far from Portsmouth. That's where James is now. At least that's where he was or was near, when he wrote his last letter.

How's the East Coast and Camp Lee? You always said you wanted to visit the East Coast. You've been almost all over the rest of the U.S. I'll bet you didn't expect to do it quite like this. To tell the truth, neither did I. You said Camp Lee was supposed to be the largest Quarter Master's Camp in the world. What are you doing there? You going to be a Quarter Master? Kenneth King is a 1st Lieutenant in the Q.M. - he's stationed in North Carolina somewhere.

Did you have a nice Easter? We had lovely weather here. We didn't go anywhere. Just stayed home. I'll take that back – we didn't stay home. We went to church in the morning and when we got home and ate dinner we went to Newgulf. Mother and Dad went to a funeral, but I stayed at Aunt Frances' and helped take care of some little kids. The funeral was that of Mr. Geo. Shwebel. I'm sure you remember him. The Schwebel's were our neighbors to the right when we lived in Newgulf. The Red Cross managed to get leaves for both of his sailor sons. Shelby, his youngest son, flew in from the South Pacific so he could be with him. I think it's wonderful how the Red Cross can be depended on in the time of need. Both of the boys' leaves were extended so they could be here when he died. The doctors knew he couldn't live. He died Saturday morning at 6:30 and was buried in Wharton yesterday, Easter Sunday.

We got a letter from Ann the same day we got your card. As you probably already know everything in Houston is fine. I'm going up and spend the weekend either this coming or the following weekend.

Mother and Dad are fine. Mother said she would write you a long letter tomorrow. Right now she's out in the garden getting ready to plant seeds. Grandma's here and out helping her and that's where I'm going when I'm finished here. Dad's got the garden all plowed and fixed so it won't be much more than just digging holes and putting the seeds in.

By the way, are you situated where you can receive packages? Don't forget to tell me. If you don't "You'll be sorry".

I guess I'd better go out and put a few seeds in the ground.

Love,

Sis

April 11, 1944 – from Ann, Missouri Ave, Houston, to Camp Lee, VA

Tuesday A.M.

Hi Sweet,

Last night I went to Dorothy and Van's. Picked up Norma. Had a farewell drink and I wanted to cry – so did Norma – you know us! Norma's leaving on the bus Thursday for St. Pete. I'll tell you all about it tonight. Van leaves in the morning – April 12 – remember?

I suppose by now Doris knows you're there. Pat and Tommie Cummins are up there too – So are Jim Wilson and his wife – small world, eh?

This is going to be short and snappy, sweetheart because it's almost time for the mail man. Thought I'd drop a line to Doris too and will write you again tonight. I'm going to drop a hint to her for an invitation for a visit! I'm coming up, babe! Let me know how long you expect to be there and everything.

I love you –

Baby

P.S.: We're both well.

April 12, 1944 – from Ann, Missouri Ave, Houston, to Camp Lee, VA

Tuesday PM

Dearest,

I wrote this morning but thought I'd write a little longer tonight. I talked to Van today and gave him your address. He said he'd write just as soon as he could. He's leaving at seven in the morning. Saw Kirk and Mrs. K last night.

Wednesday

I had to stop last night because the baby woke up just as I started the letter. I put her in my bed and she slept all night with me. I guess she was dreaming. Anyway, I saw Mrs. K last night again. Same old stuff!

I've been sewing. That's why my letters haven't been as long as they were. And too I just haven't any knowledge of what you're doing or anything so I can't very well discuss anything with you. Please write and tell me all about yourself. I hope (if you're going to stay there very long) to come up there.

I'm sure Doris would put me up. I'm going to write her today and I'm not putting it off a minute. I received a letter from Sis yesterday. I think she's going to come up for a week – and pretty soon.

I talked to Ralph the other morning but haven't seen him since last Friday. Everyone is well now so I guess we'll be able to start visiting. I'm going now sweet, so until tonight – bye now!

I love you always,

Baby

April 12, 1944 – from Ann, on their fourth wedding anniversary - from Missouri Ave, Houston, to Camp Lee, VA

This envelope from Ann contains two letters, the first on the back of a blue receipt from Tidy Didy Wash, Sterilized Diaper Service. 47 diapers cost $1.50 to wash!
Ore Nell Brandt is Bill's 19 year old cousin. Edna Emma Brandt Witt, 28, is another cousin (the daughter of Tillie's younger brother Arthur Hilbert Brandt, and Kathleen refers to Edna's daughter (Cathleen Witt Dunne) who is 9 months old at the time. I am unsure who Nate is, possibly another cousin.

Dearest,

Ralph just came by for me – he couldn't find a place so I showed him. I'm sitting out in the car now so that's the reason for the stationery. Fine stuff, eh and got a letter from Ore Nell today, she says Edna and Kathleen both have measles and all of Nate's kids have it, too. She's (Ore Nell is) in love again! It really sounds like its serious! Hope so. I was hoping I'd get a letter from my husband of 4 years today, but I didn't. I hope you've seen Doris. I suppose you have. If I can weedle an invitation out of her, your bride of 4 years and your daughter of 18 months will be saying hi-ho before you know it. When I know how long your basic will be, I can make more definite plans. Then maybe in a couple of weeks you'll get a wire stating arrival time of your two gals. Wish we could be together tonight. I know I've missed you but I'll be more lonesome tonight than ever. I'm sewing – trying to build up a wardrobe for my second honeymoon. Will write more later.

I love you.

Dearest one,

Here I am again. The little blue slip was written while waiting for Ralph. He made the sale! She paid one whole year! Swell, isn't it? He said I brought him good luck. He stayed for dinner and left soon after because he had an appointment. Swell kid. Did you get the letter about his eyes? I want you to be sure and have yours checked. That scar business can be serious – it may be the cause of the feeling of sand in your eyes – please fix 'em up. I'm going to write Doris right now so guess you two will get the letters at the same time. I also want to know about Army etiquette – is it alright or permissible for a private's wife to visit an officer's home? Of course, Doris hasn't said anything about my coming up but I'm going to do some hinting!

Hope I get a letter tomorrow. Then I'll be able to write a little more. Oh yes, I went by to see Henrietta today – her baby is precious. He was sleeping but he looks precious. Van left this morning and Norma is leaving tomorrow. I hope I can say I'm leaving pretty soon – don't you? Or do you? What do you think about it – do you like the idea?

I want to get back to my sewing and I've got to write Doris so I'd better go. Be sweet and try air mail sometime – it takes 6 to 7 days for a letter to get to me.

I love you all my life and I'd love to spend one hour with you tonight –

Yours,

Baby

April 14, 1944 – William and Matilda Genzer (Bill's parents) from Newgulf, TX
To: Pvt. William A. Genzer
A.S.N. 38671305
1st Platoon
Co. "O", 7th Q.M.T.R.
Camp Lee, Virginia

There are several misspelled words which were corrected to make it easier to read.

Friday, noon the 14th

Dearest Son,

Hear I go writing you a few lines. How are you in your new camp, hope you are alright and well. We are all well and doing the best we can. What are you doing by now? Have you got any special work or what. Tell us all about it if you can, we just got your card, you wrote when you got there.

How is the weather out there, it is really pretty here now. In fact, it is getting dry now. When we plant anything, we have to water it and potatoes we are going to plant in dry today, it is later for potatoes but we are going to try it and see if they will make yet. We got a few tomatoes and cabbage set out and planted some other seed but had to put some water on it so it will come up. The reason it is dry now because we didn't get to plow until after all that rain and now all the loose grown dried out.

I heard from Ann and Carol the other day and they all were just fine. I guess Sis will write you in a day or so, she knows more what to write than I do. I guess you will think my letters are awful short, but I will write as often as I can, if it isn't much, just so you hear from us all.

And you write as often (as) you can. I must close now and mail this so you get it.

You be good and much love from us,

Mom & Pop

April 15, 1944 – from Missouri Ave, Houston, TX, to Camp Lee, VA

Friday p.m.

Hello sweet,

Golly it was so swell to hear from you. Honey, I don't care whether you write a letter or not – just a note saying you're OK. That "letter" from you today gave me some idea of what you're doing anyway. I'd kinda like to know a little more, tho.

Same old stuff – nothing exciting. The baby is fine – thank goodness! I have a swell surprise for you but it'll be about three weeks yet before I can send them. Maybe, if I ever hear from you about your feeling of my visiting (?) with you – maybe I can bring them by then! Hope so!

Mr. & Mrs. Lorris came by for me last night and we took Norma to the bus station. The bus was due at 8:45 to leave – she got away at 9:30! I'll never ride the busses. I think I could do much better on the train. I think I will take the train in a couple of weeks! How's that? Jean wants me to go to Lafayette with her next Thursday. Theo is going down and we'd come back Sunday night. Then the next week I hope to get to Newgulf. Then when I come back I'll be ready to go to Virginia! I wish you would write and let me know how you feel. I want to be with you more than anything. Next best thing to having you with me is to have a few snaps of my love – how about it?

Just finished listening to "I Love a Mystery" – darn good story, too!

Well sweet, I'd better close now and go up. I've been sewing all day – all I have to do is put in the hem and I'll be through – It's green with white trimmings (*Ann draws a picture of what the dress looks like*) – How do you like it?

Will write more tomorrow – I love you all my life – write soon.

Forever Yours,

Mommy

P.S.: Received a letter from Max. Here's his address – when you have a moment drop him a line – Pvt. A.M. Groves, ASN 18118697, 20th Tech. S. Sq., Lowry, Field, Colorado

---

April 16, 1944 – from Missouri Ave, Houston, TX, to Camp Lee, VA

Saturday p.m.

Sweetheart,

How's everything? Hope fine. Jean and Anna Louise and I are going to the show in just a few minutes and so this will probably be a short one.

I did want to tell you though that our squirt has almost graduated! Yes, she's chewing gum now! And she eats candy in the afternoons and cookies all day and today we went to the ice cream "joint down to the corner" and she ate a whole cone of sherbet! (Only one scoop, tho.) She asks for you every day and today we were down at the drug store having a coke and a tall boy came by and she yelled "Da-Da" – Oh boy!

Well, sweet, I'd better run so bye now – be sweet and will write lots tomorrow. I love you all my life.

Me

April 17, 1944 – from Missouri Ave, Houston, TX, to Camp Lee, VA

Inside the envelope, Ann writes: Say, what does A.S.N. mean before your serial number? Please write.

Sunday

Dearest,

Here it is – Sunday afternoon and not a thing to do. Yesterday it was so hot we nearly died! Then today we have a nice little norther to spice life a bit! Disgusting, isn't it? The chick just woke up and is walking around with a cookie in her hand. She is getting so big and her vocabulary has grown so I don't doubt she will be talking as much as Susan when you see her.

I do hope you find time soon to write me.

There are so many things I'd like to know. For instance, what do you think of the Army and do you think you will be able to get a pretty good rating? How are your chances for a Major Sgt (or Sgt Major, rather) rating? How about O.C.S.? What are you studying and training for and do you suppose we'll be able to be together at all either during or after your basic? Gosh honey, I know how this letter may sound to you. Perhaps some of the questions are a bit off but you see I don't know anything about it. I'd like to know about Doris and Joe, too. Please write – if only a few words about yourself. I'm starved for info about my man. Hope all my letters are getting to you. I haven't missed a day and have written twice on some occasions.

I've finished my dress and expect to start on another tomorrow. I only hope I'm fixing up for a trip to you.

There isn't anything more to say so I guess I'd better close. I don't suppose this letter is a very satisfactory one but if I could only hear that you're alright I'll brighten them up a bit.

Will write again tomorrow so until then, I love you and both your girls miss you terribly.

Yours forever, Baby

April 18, 1944 – from Missouri Ave, to Camp Lee, VA

Monday noon

Dearest,

Thought I'd begin this now so if I don't find time later, I'll have already written for today.

The two weeks period for the measles was up yesterday so I took the baby to the doctor for a checkup today. No sign of measles and since the epidemic has almost ceased I think we missed it. Hope so anyway. She had a sore throat, kinda red, but he gave her some medicine and he said it looked more like an allergy. It may be caused from the legustrum which is blooming now. He said her sneezing so much indicates that and would cause the irritated throat. He's so nice, honey. He takes so much interest in her. He asked about you and said he was at Camp Lee during the last war. He was a captain at the time and had charge of the mess. He was there only about 2 months. He reached a Lt. Colonel before the war ended. Let's see if you can top him (Ain't I the funny one, tho!)

It's just about time for the mail man so here's hoping I'll be happy over hearing from my favorite soldier! Oh boy, you should hear some of my dreams! I had the R.A.'s yesterday and when I went to bed it seemed I missed you more than ever. I guess I just fell to sleep and kept on dreaming of you. Did you dream of me, too, last night? Sunday night – the 24th? Let me know – it would be funny if we were really together last night, wouldn't it? I really feel as though we were and I feel pretty good today because of it.

Polly Boehme just called. She wants me for tea Thursday afternoon at 4 p.m. I told her I'd be delighted. She's going to ask Mrs. K., so I guess we'll go together. I'm on this month's IBM Wives committee so I'm going to have to get in touch with the girls soon and start planning something.

I talked to Henrietta this a.m. Charles' best friend was killed out at the South Main Airport in a crash landing yesterday. Two women were with him. Students – she said if that had had their license, he (Chas) would have been flying with him. She said she didn't have the shakes, she had the jerks! Poor kid!

I got our license. They cost $11.31 or thereabouts. And I have the bank book balanced perfectly with the statement. I'm getting into our reserve now because my allotment hasn't shown up yet for April. I want you to wire FDR of this matter immediately! I'm doing pretty good, tho, and am just a little proud of myself, too - aren't you?

By the way, if you run across a decent fountain pen at the P.X., I wish you'd send it to me. I'll reimburse you immediately! No kidding, this dear old thing is positively shot! Remember, I like a <u>blunt</u> point.

The mail man just arrived. A letter from Giggs, a card from Mary Elizabeth congratulating us on our fourth year and a copy of your life insurance with the government. And still no letter from you. Really, I don't think a card of a few words would be so hard to find time for. I'm sorry. I don't mean to be nasty but I can't help but feel just a wee hurt.

I felt good this morning. I was so sure you were going to have a letter in my box for me today – I hope you're getting my letters because I don't want you to feel any disappointment. I'm going to go now. Think I'll sew awhile. Be good – and remember I told you in a letter of last week to try Air-Mail sometime – well, babe, let's change that to – try mail sometime!

I love you so much it hurts,

Your baby

April 18, 1944 – from Lorraine Genzer, Newgulf, TX, to Camp Lee, VA

Aunt Agnes is Bill's father's older sister, Agnes Genzer, and Uncle Joe Papacek is most likely her husband. I am unsure of Aunt Frances' relationship, but she may be married to one of William Genzer's brothers.
Uncle Fritz is Willie's younger brother, 46.
Grandma refers to Agnes Knapik Genzer, Willie's mother, 75.

April 17, 1944

Dear Bill,

How's Virginia after almost two weeks? Of course, I wouldn't know. I've never been there and I haven't received any letters from there. I couldn't be hinting, of course, you know that. What's the matter anyway. Have you been that busy or have you just forgotten you have a little sis back home.

As usual and always, things around here are still the same. I wouldn't know what to do if they were to change. Aunt Agnes and Uncle Joe Papacek were here yesterday. It's been almost four years since I'd seen them. Venice and her husband, Robert Soligar, came with them. It's been seven years since she's been down here. She has really changed. I don't believe you'd know her if you were to see her. Aunt Frances, Uncle Fritz, Millie, Jerry and Grandpa Shinek and Grandma were here too and we all had dinner here and talked and visited. We really had a house full. Pop called Ann and wanted her to come but she said the doctor said it would better for Carol to stay in since there are so many cases of measles going around. Henrietta was the same way so neither of them were able to be here and we really missed them.

Well, we finally got our telephone. At least it's on the wall – it isn't connected yet though. Pop brought it home Saturday and hung it up. He said even if it doesn't work yet we can fool everybody. All it needs is to be connected to the line. We'll probably get that done sometime this week. I can hardly wait. It will seem as if we're a little closer in town even if we really aren't.

Bill, you know Mother's Day isn't far off – well, Pop and I really have things planned for Mom. You know she doesn't have a dresser or vanity or anything in her room, well, we're getting her one. She doesn't even suspect. It's really a dressing table. Pop spotted a beautiful huge mirror that originally cost $40 and he can get it for $20. It's in perfect condition but it belongs to a fellow who's going into the Army and who is trying to get rid of his things. He's, Pop, is going to get that and either make or buy the table and I'm going to make the curtain for it. I think she'll really like it because it's something she wants and also something she needs.

That garden I wrote you about in my last letter is coming up nicely and it surely looks pretty. We have the garden in the front where we had potatoes last year and potatoes where we had the garden last year. We just swapped.

Guess what? What do you think Mother will do next? She caught a swarm of bees last week. She said she heard them coming so she got a sweep and a hoe and started banging them together and they came down and gathered and hung on one of the peach trees. When Pop came home, he put them in a box built a real hive and trap the next day and then traded boxes. You might know that while he was trading boxes with them, I'd be standing too close and one of them came and stung me right between the eyes. Boy, but was I a pretty sight. It swoll up a little but I kept bathing it in alcohol and it went down before morning. We asked Mom what she was going to get out here to raise next – a family of skunks? We expect most anything when we get home in the evenings.

Write soon and don't work <u>too</u> hard.

Love,

Sis

P.S.: Pardon for the little fussing I gave you for not writing because Pop just came in with your letter. And about that Devil's Food cake – I'll see what I can do.

April 19, 1944 – from Missouri Ave, Houston, TX, to Camp Lee, VA

Oh my sweet!

I received that grand long letter from you today so am sending this air mail so you won't feel bad about those letters of yesterday and the day before. I had fully made up my mind to send you a night message. I was thinking all sorts of things – measles, typhoid, or another awful disease had you in its clutches! And speaking of stuff like that – the baby is all over her sore throat and I feel wonderful since the mail man arrived!

I had so many things to tell you and now I can't think of a thing. I'll just start talking – I mean – writing and maybe the news will just pop out.

Ah – a thought! Tell me all about Doris and Joe. Then about you and your doings and don't forget to look for the fountain pen at the P.X. and Theo's cigarette lighter, too. He was here for dinner tonight and told me to be sure to remind you of it.

I talked to Dorothy last night. She's holding the fort down exceptionally well. Van's in San Diego. He arrived there Sunday morning.

Mrs. K. called this evening for a game of bridge. I didn't feel up to it. Then Jean called. Lou's in

Lafayette – working there now – and he called her. She said Bobbie and the two kids spent the day with Aunt Odette and Daddy laid off to be with them. A big party! I bet!

I'm listening to the radio and writing during music and advertisements! Fine stuff, huh?

It's a shame you didn't get to see Washington - How far is it from camp, and how would you like to visit Washington with your wife and chicken? Huh? How about answering that, babe!

I don't have a darn thing to talk about except my sewing and our chicken. My sewing is fine. I'm on a blue and white striped princess dress now – it's cute. Hope you like my two dresses, and as for our little "he-be" – she's keeping me jumping! We missed you terribly April 12, but not as much as last night – I feel pretty swell today though. I'm looking kinda good too even if I say so myself! Weight 107 – waistline 26! Purty good for your freckled face fat baby – huh?

I've got a swell surprise for you. I'll send them just as soon as they get here. Probably another couple of weeks though – Ha, I bet you're dying of curiosity!

Well, sweet, I guess I'd better close now. I love you to pieces and I miss you – wouldn't you?

Bye now,

Love and kisses – Yours,

Mommy

P.S.: Had to buy a new battery today. They made a settlement – got a $9.50 battery for $5.27 – 24 year guarantee – the best they had! How'm I doing?

April 20, 1944 – from Missouri Ave, to Camp Lee, VA

Hello sweetheart,

Just received your letter asking for a list of things. It was so swell to hear from you a second time in succession! Really was swell.

You know, honey, we've had something these four years – that something has been honesty – complete honesty. If a thought hits me, I'm going to express it because I know you'll be completely honest with me as to your reactions. Naturally, I'd love to be with you, but I didn't think about it too much until I had heard from you – about coming up there, I mean. I knew that you'd be unable to live off the post, besides being expensive on what we're trying to live on, so I'm not disappointed, sweet. If I hadn't thought you would tell me if it wasn't a practical idea, I would never have mentioned it. I know this too – that when the time comes when you're able to have us, you'll lose no time in telling me. That's why we miss each other more than the average couple, our marriage wasn't based on just love, it was based on love and a grand friendship – you see we like each other just as much as we love one another. Gee – what a lecture for a 5-footer!

Now, sweetheart, I want to know something. When you left here, you wore a size 34 short – and you also had a cold. Now, you ask for size 32 – have you lost? Have you been sick? It costs 8¢ to send an Air Mail but since I have just 3¢ ones, here on hand, I'll enclose three. Please let me know 'cause I want to know.

I'm going to town tomorrow, so will get requested articles for you then. I can't make any cookies until next week, but just as soon as I get the sugar will make my soldier some lovely burnt cookies like I always make!

Have you any close friends up there? Let me know all about it! I'm so curious to find out everything about Army Life.

Henrietta, Chas, the baby, Carol and I are going to Newgulf Friday. I'm trying to get Ralph to go. He says it's pretty hard for him to leave before Sat. noon, but I hope he gets to go. Wish my guy were here to go with us.

I talked to Granny just a while ago. She hasn't heard from Doris but was thrilled to hear you'd seen them.

I guess I'd better quit now and go fix the chicken's dinner. Dr. Wallis has me skipping around on menus and the exema is almost clear!

I just put her to bed, so will now explain the above statement. He doesn't want me to give her any foods two days in succession. Like if – well, I'll give you two days menus:

Brkfast – oatmeal, prunes, toast
Lunch – Potatoes, string beans, lamb chop, jello
Dinner – Milk toast, fruit (different from morn), bacon and cookie with the rest of her milk

2nd day –
Brkfst – oatmeal, prunes, toast, bacon
Lunch – Liver broiled, noodles, and veg. soup, fruit (different from morn & yesterday's supper & lunch)
Dinner – Grits and beef gravy, jello, toast

See? Pretty good, eh – she's eating milk toast and grits and crackers, milk with vanilla and sugar and all sorts of good stuff (but light) at night. She eats beef and chicken and lamb chops and bacon now and is getting along fine. Between meals she gets hard candies and gum! Imagine a doctor prescribing gum! Fine, eh? She swallows it if I don't keep after her but she has to learn so I keep after her. Please send us a picture of our Daddy. She is still calling for you and looking for you mornings and evenings. This evening, she was sleepy and wanted you. I could have bawled! But we're doing fine, sweet.

I saw "Lady in the Dark" last week. Be sure to see it if you can. Ray Milland and Ginger Rogers and it's just grand. Notice the clothes! Yum, yum! And speaking of shows, I think I'll go to the Tower. Ants, you know, in the dear old pants - !

I'll write again tomorrow and will send everything including A.M. stamps – Bye now. I adore you, my sweet, so take care of "Our Bill" for your baby and me.

I love you all my life,

Yours,

Baby

April 20, 1944 – sister Lorraine Genzer from Newgulf, TX

Dear Bill,

This is just a note to let you know you have a package coming. Don't get scared when you see it because it won't bite. I decorated it up like that because I didn't want it to get bounced around too much.

Don't mind the way it's picked, that's Pop's way of getting it there without getting messed up. You may need a crow-bar to get in but after you're once in, I hope you're not disappointed. If it's good and arrived in good condition, let me know and I'll send another later. OK?

Here's hoping <u>it's</u> good –

Love,

Sis

P.S.: Do you by chance like Divinity and Chocolate Fudge? Huh?

April 21, 1944 – from Missouri Ave, Houston, to Camp Lee, VA

Thursday p.m.

Hello sweet,

This is going to be short because I'm worn to a frazzle! Just finished my blue dress so I can take it to Newgulf with me in the morning. We're leaving about 9, so I'll have plenty to do in the morning without sewing. It's kinda late and I have to bathe. My country cousin showed up yesterday. I was a little worried there for awhile – should have been here around the 13th and here it shows up on the 20th!

The baby is fine and talks of going "bye bye to see Momo and Popeye" – she's really getting to talk.

I went to Polly's for tea today – very boring affair! Lovely food but oh!, the conversation! Polly was the only one there whom I'd met before. About 12 were there so you can imagine what a dull hour I spent.

I'll write from HOME tomorrow and will tell you all about it. Forgive this short note but I'll make up for it tomorrow night. Oh, yes, I got the shorts and things but can't send there until Saturday because tomorrow's the 21st – San Jacinto Day.

Be sweet and I love you terribly much. Take care of yourself and don't think too much about that furlough – it might cause mental telepathy and my dreams are enough of a wow now! By the way, you've never told me what you dreamed that Sunday night – Easter Sunday nite, I believe. Tell me, it'd be fun to compare.

I love you all my life,

Baby

April 21, 1944 (postmark on letter) – from Pvt. A.E. Genzer, A.S.N. 38554290, Co. A 78th Engineer Bn., A.P.O. 847, c/o Postmaster, Miami, FL
Via U.S. Army Postal Service, postmarked May 30, 1944

This letter is from Bill's first cousin, Alfred Emil "Slim" Genzer, known as Fred, son of Joseph Genzer Jr., William Genzer's older brother. Fred is 19 years old at the time he writes this letter.

April 20, 1944
Puerto Rico

Dear Bill,

Just a few lines while I have a few minutes to spare.

How are you getting along, hope fine. And how do you like the army. I hope fine. I am pretty good myself.

I am somewhere in Puerto Rico. It's really nice here. I was an M.P., but now I am in the engineers. It's pretty good.

I guess you wonder how I got your address. Well, your sister send it to me. I was surprise to hear that you are in the army. You must be in the quartermasters. Its some boys here that was at Camp Lee. They say it's a pretty nice place. Well, I wish I was back in the states. But I have 22 more months before I'll get back.

I was going to the show but I saw the picture before.

You might not read this scratching. I am writing on my knee. A person learns to write anywhere in this army.

Well, I hate to do this but I'll have to close for this time. So good bye and good luck until next time.

Your cousin, Fred

April 22, 1944 – from Wharton

Friday

Dearest, oh boy can I spell!

Here I am in Cottondale. Chas, Henry, their baby, Carol and I arrived in Newgulf about noon. Everyone's fine and I hope the cake arrived safely. Pop put it in a wooden box so I hope you didn't think it was a bomb! I want to send you some cookies so be sure to let me know how long it took.

Sis went to the show with Bobbie and Mom and Pop are feeding. Grandma is here on the porch with me. She said she wished you could have kuloches *(?)* because she would surely make some for you. I just put Carol in your Mother's bed. She's already asleep. I'm going to move her later because we have no baby bed so she's going to sleep with me. Hope she sleeps well. Mom just came in so I guess we'll eat. We're having chili – wouldn't you care to join us?

I'm going to fix up the package and send it in the morning. We're going to Wharton. I have everything you asked for with a few additional coat-hangers. Hope the shorts and undershirts are right. If not, I can exchange them.

By the way, did you ever have your eyelids examined? I wish you would. If you see about it now you may escape a painful procedure in later years. Let me know about it.

James Armstrong, a boyfriend of Sis', is somewhere near you and will plan to look you up. She is going to send your number (what does A.S.N. mean?), so he can find you.

Have you seen much of Doris and Joe? I wish you'd say more about them. I'd like to know the set up.

Nothing special to talk about so I hope this won't be boring.

I expect to leave Sunday afternoon and return in a few weeks for a long visit. I think I'll go out to Bobbie's and stay a few days with her this week. Theo reserved a drawing room for them to come back on the train. Hope they escape the measles. The folks at LaGrange are all on the mend, thank goodness, but we're staying away from there anyway!

Tell me all about what you're doing and here's something I'd like to know – you know nothing about tab machines – will they change your classification or does that mean further training? And another thing – has the Kelley field business fallen through or do you still have a chance? I suggest you burn this – I'd hate to queer anything at this late date – or is it early? I guess it is!

Your surprise hasn't arrived yet but when it does, I'll air-mail it to you. I know you'll adore it and prize it forever. Hope so anyway – getting curious? Ha, ha!

I still haven't my allotment – have you ever gotten paid? It's worried me because I thought when you received your paycheck I'd get the bond you bought – don't you think? Or do they do that?

Listen honey, do you have the Q.M. insignia on your uniform? I saw the emblem tonight and I'd surely like to have a pin like it.

Speaking of pens, did you look for one for me at the P.X.? How about Theo's lighter? If you do this for me I'll do something real nice for you – how about it?

We just finished eating and we're being very stylish. Eating by candlelight! Not cause we want to, you understand, but because we're forced to! You see, there's about 6 hours on one circuit and Mr. King's electric milking equipment is forever shorting it so here we sit in the dark. It won't be too long though because it's almost ten o'clock and we'll be going to bed soon. Pop is on the couch already snoring and my eyes need props. Busy day for all of us. The squirt is sleeping away. I hope she doesn't wake up when I move her. Sweet little doll. We went over to Grandma's to get her this evening and she saw your picture on the dresser – she (Carol) rushed over and squealed "Da Da!" Grandma nearly fainted. She's still talking about it. She was walking around with your picture this noon and just kissing it and getting Mom and I to kiss it too. You just have to get one made for us. I want one for the bureau and one for my billfold – so please! Mom says she wants one too. I'm going to have to close now – this 2 power candlelight isn't helping my eyes any, so will close and say I love you – keep yourself for me.

Love and Kisses,

Mommy

P.S.: If you can't get razor blades I'll send some. I didn't think of them until I started packing so let me know. I'm being mean as hell but am keeping fine for you. Say, kid, since when have I been living at 1204 Missouri? Notice return address for correction!

I love you all my life.

April 24, 1944 – from Missouri Ave, Houston, to Camp Lee, VA

Sunday

Hello my darling,

Please excuse no letter on Saturday night. I really was sorry but, Honey, Mom, Sis, and I went to Wharton to the show and you know how one of those juicy double features are. Talk about paralyzed tail bones! (Remember?) We got home about 12:30 and the dog woke up the baby barking so I had to go in and put her back to sleep. By then I was too so there went my boy's letter! Am I forgiven?

We got home about 9:30. The chick went to sleep right out of Newgulf and hasn't waked up yet! It's almost ten now so this won't be long. I'm enclosing a letter from Mr. Packard and a booklet the company sent.

Everything's fine. The baby's well and so am I. Granny got a letter from Doris and she said after your 3 weeks of basic is over they're going to see a lot of you. The lucky dogs!

Sister, your Mom and all of us got to talking about your furlough. Pop said he was going to send you money for a compartment so you wouldn't be so tired when you got home. Well, Mom said she thought since it would be around $40 or $50 you could add your train fare and fly if you didn't mind planes – I said you'd love it so she said to please ask you what you thought of it – what say, babe?

I'm going to close now so I can get a little shut eye so be sweet and I adore you and miss you more and more. Please keep loving me and your chick –

Kisses and hugs,

Your baby

P.S.: Packard's letter came Air Mail! Oh yes, am enclosing some A.M. Stamps. I love you – B.

April 25, 1944 – from Missouri Ave, Houston, to Camp Lee, VA

Eli may refer to another house helper.

Monday

Hello sweet,

It seems all during the day I have so many things to tell you that I know I'll have a long letter to send my lover but when I start writing it all leaves me. Well, I'll start with this.

Johnny Carter called today. He wanted me to see if your last check was correct. As I figure it, it was. Then he told me to tell you that he had corresponded quite a few times with Rochester and they found they had paid you the four hours overtime on your July 26 check but dated it week ending June 30. This was a duplication. Hope you understand. I didn't know anything about it but he said you knew and he was sending your statements to me.

And another thing, I forgot to enclose the booklet and letter from Mr. Packard. That's how nutty I am.

Mama, Louise, and Eli are cleaning up this week. They have really been working. Got Aunt Odette's vacuum (the one you fixed) and cleaned the walls, took down the curtains for washing, vacuumed the upholstered chair and wicker furniture. I hope the flu bugs are gone now.

Jean just came in. She's going to Lafayette tonight. I don't envy her the trip, she leaves at 11:30 tonite and arrived at 5:30 in the morning! Bobbie and the two kids are coming in tonight and Daddy's coming with them. Theo and Mama have gone to the station now. I'm quitting now to take the squirt upstairs to bed. I'm not going to bathe her tonight because it's too cold. Just going to dip her in the basin! Poor baby! Bye now – see you later.

8 p.m. and all's well – the chick's in bed and it's quiet as hell.

It's so swell to hear from you. Received the card today and although I'd rather hear more, it makes me feel so good to hear from you. It makes us close or sumpin'! I know I look forward every day to writing you that night because it seems like I'm really talking to you and when you've told me somethings, I can talk with you about them. It sure helps to keep Old Man Blues away.

Which reminds me – I think I'll go call Dorothy – see you later. Well, that was quick – she must not be at home. Probably over at her Mother's. I tried to get Mrs. Lorris too but her line was busy. I heard from Norma. She arrived in St. Pete OK and Tommie gets to be with her almost every weekend. Isn't that swell? He's on a boat and St. P is his home port. I hope we're as lucky as they. And when I talked with Johnny today he said Tully (is that right?) is still in S.A. He left about a week after you did.

Say, bud, you know how much our telephone bill is this month - $12.02! I could have gone to S.A. and back on that – and I wouldn't mind seeing a charge from Camp Lee when a certain guy felt like he'd like 3 min with a voice I hope he loves.

Hope you received the Air Mail stamps alright. I'm not going to forget to enclose the others. I'm going to end this now as it'll cost more if I don't so write when you can.

I love you all my life –

With all my love –

Your baby

April 26, 1944 – from Missouri Ave, Houston, to Camp Lee, VA

The "two kids" Ann refers to are Dianne, 4, and Susan, 2, Bobbie and Theo's daughters.
Odette, 48, is married to Grover Ernest Mouton, 49, a younger brother of Ann's mother. Lou refers to Leufroy Joseph Burguierres Mouton, 26, Odette and Grover's second son. Jeanne is Lou's wife, Jeanne Shockley Mouton, 23, who is Odette's daughter-in-law. Also, Maria?
Aunt Hattie, 48, is Sarah Ann Mouton Quattlebaum's younger sister, Mary Harriet Mouton Williams.

Tuesday P.M.

Hiya popsy,

Well, we have really had a day! I'll begin with last night – Bobbie, Daddy and the two kids arrived about 8:30. Jean came by saying she was leaving on the 11:30 train so we said we'd take her. After the cyclone came and went we talked until 10:30, then Daddy and I drove Jean and Ann to the station. We didn't get home until about 11:45. Carol woke up about 7am and today started! Carita came in – she drove up by herself - and Benton's driving Mama's car up Friday. Daddy's leaving in the morning and B & C are leaving Sunday on their way to Okla. They're to see that allergy specialist. I was thinking of going back to LA with them but they're driving straight up to Oklahoma from here. We went over to Bobbie's today and spent the afternoon. Bobbie's worn out. She said when they got up this morning she put on dirty dresses and they fooled around all they wanted. You know the dress-up situation in Crowley. Bobbie said she had a gorgeous time but boy was she glad to be home! She looks like she's gained five pounds – and speaking of people gaining: I forgot to tell you – Jean is pregnant.

She went to see Dr. Gardner Saturday and he confirmed it. The baby's due the latter part of November. I'll bet the little kid gets here before though because she's as big as I was at 4 months. Aunt Odette is out of this world and I can imagine how Lou feels. How about you – would you like to get a letter from me saying something like that? How's about it?

Daddy's sitting with me down here in the sunroom reading the family tree of the Louailliers. I'm just putting in the rest of the baby's family tree in her book. He put that down and is looking over her baby book now. Carita, Maria and Aunt Tennie are upstairs and we expect to join them when I finish this. That sweet little hunk of heaven of ours is really snoozing away!

I talked with Dorothy this morning and got Van's address. He seems to be doing pretty well although he's plenty lonesome. Dorothy said he signed his last letter – "To the sweetest family a guy could possibly have" – she was about to cry!

Say, I hate to keep mentioning it, but I've never heard from you one word about a fountain pen (with a blunt point) and a cigarette lighter for one Theo Frank. By the way, Janet and Theo Sr., heard from Jack Russel. He's in England and is doing OK.

Aunt Hattie is not so well. She's still at it. She hasn't stopped flowing yet and you know how long it's been. She started right after Christmas. Several times she grew better but it was never checked completely. She's taking x-ray treatments now but if they haven't done any more good than they're doing, she'll have to resort to radium. Mama's really worried about her. Her state of mine is pretty bad and she cries every time you mention B.J. I wish you'd drop them a card. It would thrill them all and be sure to say – hope Aunt Hattie is feeling much better or fine or something to that effect. I'll get B.J.'s address and you may be within seeing distance of him. I have a few other addresses I'll give to you as soon as I get them checked. I think I'd better quit now so you can get to something important (if I didn't think this was, I wouldn't write it so don't get mad.)

Until tomorrow, be sweet and both your babies miss and love you so terribly much –

Love to the sweetest daddy and husband a family could ever have –

Mommy

P.S.: Forgot to tell you – your daughter got into my Bond Street, Yardley's Cologne and now I have no more Bond Street, Yardley's Cologne – but my bedroom smells awfully sweet!

April 27, 1944 – from Missouri Ave, Houston, to Camp Lee, VA

Wednesday,
 April 26, '44

Dearest,

Received your card today about the pleasant weekend with Doris and Joe. It surely makes me feel swell to know you're with friends. I know it must make you feel good, too. She owes me a letter but if I don't hear from her by Friday or Saturday, I'll write – oh, I may dash off a "thank you" note to her tonight or tomorrow – yes, that's what I'll do. It was so good to get word today. After all the company arrived, Bobbie got sick. She has a terrific cold and looks a lot like she has the flu. Hope not! Carol is well so am staying away just on general principles.

I'm going to have the car Simonized by Eli and checked by Alfred. He's a mechanic for the Yellow Cab Co., so he must now his business. I'm going to have to have the brakes relined or something I'm sure because the fluid doesn't last as long as it should. He'll tell me the truth and as Eli puts it – he won't take your eye-balls out with the price. Benton is coming over Friday, as I told you so am going to ask him what he thinks it's worth. I'll let you know and we can decide what to do.

Sweetheart, you've never told me whether you've had your eyes checked or not. There are so many things I've asked you and you haven't answered a thing. How about it. And another thing – you say you received my letter bawling you out about not writing. Honey, you know I understand about that and if you read a letter that sounded like a bawling out, I must have been ribbing you so remember that. I know you write when you can and it thrills me to even get a card. You know this is slightly different from those two weeks we spent apart last summer! Gosh, has it been just last summer? It seems you've been gone longer than that. I miss you but won't dare tell you how much – I'd make myself start crying and anyway, <u>I</u> don't like to receive lonesome letters so I know <u>you</u> must not want them – so I'll go on writing my crazy thoughts as they come to me.

Say friend, your first wire to F.D.R. must not have done any good – better send another! I still haven't received my allotment and have only received $20.71 adj. salary and $15.00 from the company. The $15.00 was our war bond balance. I deposited that in the savings account so our checking account is really taking a beating! The insurance and doctor bills are positively robbing us. And I must soon start taking the baby for typhoid shots and Shick test and the vaccination – That's 5 visits right there besides the cost of medication! Oh boy, this business of raising a healthy child costs – but isn't it swell those visits are for a healthy child! No sir – I'm not kicking! And while we're on the subj of dough – how much does the company pay you each month and when will it start? Uh me, when you get this letter you'll wish I hadn't started in on such matters!

I'll change the subject now. Mama and Aunt Tennie went out to Bobbie's then are going out to Aunt Hattie's to pick up Carita. She spent the day there. Nice they're in C's car, eh? Anyway, I just put the squirt to bed and Betsy's coming over for gin rummy so I won't be by myself. I think she's coming now, so I'd better close. Will write a better letter tomorrow (I hope!). So long for now. Your chicken and I miss you and love you all our lives.

Kiss yourself for me.

I love you,

Mommy

Hope you get a kick out of enclosure – Here's a joke:
1st guy – I want a bastard file.   2nd guy – What size?
1st guy – I don't know. 2nd guy – I'll get some, then you can decide.
1st guy – I think I'll take that little son of a bitch over there.

Say what does A.S.F.T. mean and how does that change your status?

Bye again,

Me

April 28, 1944 – from Missouri Ave, Houston, to Camp Lee, VA

Thursday,
27 April '44

Hello Sweetheart,

Golly, another day! During the day I talk to you and say just wait until I tell you this or that and it seems to make everything OK.

First, I must tell you about last night's enclosure – I'll be sure to put it in tonight – aren't I awful!

(*Enclosure reads*: "Flash News Bulletin" – It is officially reported the Jap's have taken Sal Hepatica. The U.S. War Office admits, but doubts their ability to hold it. A late dispatch states that the strain on the rear is tremendous. The U.S. has caught them several times trying to evacuate along the line. Several flank movements have been undertaken. While the action at times remains only gas attacks. The Jap's tried to suppress the report, but it leaked out and the Allies got word of it. The Jap's now realize the value of a scrap of paper.)

(*Also enclosed – Statement from American National Insurance Co., Galveston, TX – Prepared for W. A.Genzer. Facts and Figures on Educational Policy at age 1 maturing at age 18.)*

Secondly, this is really good! Yesterday, our sweet little girl "blew a kiss" for the first time! Betsy was over here with Karen and she told her to throw Carol a kiss. She put the back of her hand to her mouth and Betsy was so proud – then Carol puts her fingers to her mouth, kisses them, and throws her hand out! I nearly bursted with pride. Betsy nearly died! Then – yesterday was the first time for this – she blew her nose! She had been playing outside and when I brought her in to put her on the toilet she took a piece of toilet paper (as usual) and sneezed about that time. I told her to blow her nose and she put the paper (it was a very little piece) and blew out of her nose and showered both of us. She hasn't forgotten either because you know how often she sneezes – well, every time now she has to blow her nose! Our baby is fast becoming a little girl!

Louise Partin called me today. She got back from Oklahoma last weekend. Charles hasn't gone overseas yet but he's in Gulfport, Mississippi taking a 4 ½ month course for Emergency Life Saving – you know – he goes out in a small boat to pick up fallen flyers and men in life boats –get it? Anyway, when he finished he'll go for sure! (My, what school did I go to!)

Bobbie is much better. Mama stayed out there with her today. Then after dinner we went out to get Carita from Aunt Hattie's. I put the chick to bed and Benton called! From Uncle Ben's! They went on out and Aunt Tennie went to bed and here I sit! Doing what I'd rather do than almost anything but tell him these things in person!

Say, bud, how's about letting me in on a few things – what does A.S.F.T.R. mean? I asked you before <u>but</u> no soap! Hope I get a letter tomorrow.

Listen honey, I wonder if I should have power of attorney for you. Dorothy has and I was wondering if I should.

And by the way – I'm enclosing the paper Ralph had fixed up for you to see what policy I meant for the baby. Hope you like it – I think it's plenty good.

That's about all for tonight, I guess – only this – every night a lighthouse keeper went to bed at 9:30 – at 10:00 a bell went bong!!! He kept on sleeping one night. One night he went to bed as usual and at 10:00 the bell didn't go bong!! He woke up and said "What's that?" – Ha – see I'm slipping – oh boy, what I would give for you to reach down and wop me one for that! (And then you could hold me in your arms!)

Tell Doris and Joe hi for me. I'm writing to them tonight. I'm so glad you're with someone you like. It sure makes me feel swell – no kiddin'.

I'm closing now, sweet, so be good and love me and your little chick.

I love you all my life,

Your baby

April 29, 1944 – from Missouri Ave, Houston, to Camp Lee, VA

Friday - 4/28/44

My darling,

I just got back from "Whistling in Brooklyn" with Red Shelton at the River Oaks. I almost turned at Mrs. Baird's Bakery to go "Home". It made me feel kinda funny. I've missed you an awful lot today. I won't say anymore because I guess you know the feeling only too well.

I bathed the baby and put her to bed, then called Mrs. Roos and we went together – golly, I've got bed on the brain – I guess I'm sleepy.

Wrote Doris last night and received a letter from her today. She said you all had a grand time over the weekend and hoped it wouldn't be too long before we'd all be together again. Here's hoping, sweet!

Still no dough from the government. None from the company either – ok, golly I hope that's the only worry we'll have from this war. You know, honey, we've been so lucky and are still lucky. Hope we can always be together because even though we're separated by miles, we're not by heart. I love you and keep thinking of you constantly. I'm sorry this isn't any longer, but I promise to do better tomorrow night.

I love you all my life,

Yours,

Mommy

April 29, 1944 – from (Mrs.) Wm. Genzer, Newgulf, TX, to Camp Lee, Virginia,

Saturday noon
April 29

Dearest Son,

How are you these days, hope fine. We all are well.

We were all ways wishing if it would stop raining and now we are wishing it would rain a little, it is dry already won't anything come up. I plant unless I water it and you know that is a job. But I guess it will rain when it get ready and it be all right.

I guess Ann wrote you that she and baby were here last weekend and we really were glad. She came up with Henerettie and her husband.

She was coming with them again this week and spend a week. But her daddy was coming home and some more folks. So she said she will come sometime later. She called Pop yesterday and told him.

We really do like for her and baby to come to see us and stay as long as she want to she is always welcome.

We bought baby a bed when she was hear so we would have one here when they come over.

By the way, did you get that cake we send you didn't hear from you in a long time.

We got a letter from Grandpa yesterday he said he can't keep up with you he said the first letter he got from you from San Antonio they from St. Louis and then from Washington D.C.

So do write him so he know where you are he like to get letters from you. And so do we. How is the country up there is it pretty like Texas. But I guess Texas is the best country yet isn't it. We have just about got our phone all fixed got the box in and post in and now working on the line. Pop said we will have it ready by the first. I think it will be handy out here.

Well, I must close and get ready and go to Wharton when Pop gets home he is going to work on the phone line some more.

Love from us all,

Mom, Pop and Sis

April 30, 1944 – from Missouri Ave, Houston, to Camp Lee, VA

Saturday

Hi Sweetheart,

Well, your chick and the old hen have had quite a day! I'll begin with our waking and will take it from there.

Carol woke up the first time about 4 this morning. I picked her up and put her in bed with me and she said "gobble-gobble-gobble-dog" and then barked like a dog – I asked her if she dreamed a dog was playing with her and she said yes. I changed her and before I could get back to bed she was sound asleep – so I don't know whether she was ever <u>really</u> awake. Anyway, I thought the incident would tickle you.

Well, then we got up at 8:00am and had breakfast and after the morning chores, Carita, Mama, Carol and I went to Bobbie's. We stayed until almost noon and then came home, at lunch, and tucked the squirt in for forty winks. Well, Benton wanted to go out to the Williams' so we went – having the baby with Louise. I came home when she woke up and then Aunt Tennie and we went on back. We had chicken (fried) and Benton cooked a delicious vegetable dish. I'm going to write it down so I can fix it for my ex-soldier when his title is that! After we ate, we came on home and I just finished putting our baby to bed. She had a grand day – slept until almost 3:30, but was awfully glad to get into bed tonight! So will this person!

This afternoon, a boyfriend of Betty's who's stationed at Ellington Field came in so we went to town and picked him up. He's an awfully nice kid but Mac's still top man. Aunt Hattie is still menstruating and isn't at all well. Mart said they received a letter from B.J. (who's in New York, by the way) and he's been assigned to a ship. When Aunt Hattie read it, she went to pieces. I'm really worried about her. She's still on the x-ray treatment but I don't see any improvement.

Benton and Carita and Mama went to get some ice cream and they just came in so I'm going to close now. Write more after they go upstairs. I Love you!

Well, they're still down here and talking, but I'm going to finish this. I'm getting kinda sleepy! You know me!

I received a star flag from the company today. It's really beautiful satin red background with a blue star on a white field. I'd surely like to see black typing on a white card, namely a check!

I'm really going to have to close now, sweet, I'm so sleepy I can barely see what I'm doing. They're finally going upstairs and by the time I finish this, they'll all be out of the bathroom so I can wash and jump in bed. Ah joy – if only I had my man – I think of your broad shoulders and shiner! And as far as your lips and arms – will I be quiet? OK, puddin'!

Be sweet and write soon. Try using those Air Mail stamps sometime. I'm out of stamps so for the next few letters you'll get will be by 3 cent stamps – I just read that last sentence! Didn't know I was that tired! So I'd better close now and go doe-doe! Bye lover – hug yourself for me. I love you and can barely wait until we're together again. Bye now –

Hugs and Kisses,

Mommy

May 1, 1944 – from Missouri Ave, Houston (on United Nations stationery), to Camp Lee, VA

Sunday, April 30, 1944

Hi Sweet,

Well, here I am out at the Frank's mansion again – recognize the stationery? We came out with Mama and Aunt Tennie this afternoon and a good time has been had by all. Carol went right to sleep but was wakened by the tornados when they retired. She turned over, snorted and grunted, gave out with a cough and went promptly back to doe-doe land! Just like her daddy at night and her Ma in the morning! I imagine I'll go home either tomorrow or the next day because I want to sew. I have some awfully pretty material – I think I can get about five pinafores out of it. It's pink – don't you love our little squirt in pink!

I went back to Dr. Griffey for a check-up finally. He said he wanted me to keep on wearing glasses for another couple of months at least. He said there was already a definite improvement in my eyes. Also that if I continued wearing them a lot, the correction would take place in a few months. By the way (I wish you would answer the questions I ask you sometime!), have you ever seen the Dr. about your eyes? I wish you'd have them checked if just to ease my mind (and don't say – what mind!)

And my friend – I'd like to know how much you weigh. When my lover left here he was sporting size 34 shorts – then (I believed I've mentioned this before but bear with me, my pet), he writes for size 32's! How about that?

Oh yes, did you receive the package alright? And how about the cake? I'm waiting on word from you as to how long it took so I can bake some cookies for you. I'll have to make some that will keep quite awhile if it takes long, but if not I can send you some Toll House cookies and some Babe Ruth cookies and how about some fudge and some homemade peanut brittle? Ha – I bet I get an answer to that question!

If I don't quit asking so many of those things, you're going to start forwarding your mail to "Information Please!"

You know, sweet, when I was over at the Williams', Betty and Martha Lee were talking about dates and running around – she said she was so glad she wasn't married so she could get out once in awhile. Well, you know me, it started me to thinking. You know, popsy, I don't know what I'd do if we weren't married. And I know even if I wasn't married, I know I just couldn't and wouldn't want to be with anybody but you and just the thought of our intimate life that has been and will be keeps me going. I think only of when we're together again.

Josephine, Louise's aunt, told my fortune today. Every time my card came up (I'm the Queen of Diamonds and you're the Jack of Diamonds), you were right behind me and we were face to face. She told me that ours was a perfect marriage and we'd always be happy – but that after this war, we were even going to be happier than we could ever conceive. And she told me another thing. We'd be together – not real soon but sooner than we think. Oh, golly, I just can't think of anything else tonight but that.

Tell Doris and Joe hello and also tell Doris I received her letter the same day I mailed one to her so I'll write this week again. It really was swell of them. I only hope we'll be able to do as much for another friend. Hope this war is over before we have that chance though.

We're all well and I hope you're not sick. The losing of the weight business has sorta made me worry. I hope it's just the exercise and early to bed, early to rise stuff!

Well, sweet, I guess I'd better be going. Bobbie's having a duck, she wants to go to bed but won't cause she's scared she'll miss something – same old Roberta! Write when you can, as much, too. Be good and keep your nose clean.

I love you,

Yours,

Mommy

May 2, 1944 – from Missouri Ave, Houston, to Camp Lee, VA

Inside the envelope, Ann writes: Remind me to tell you how much I love you sometime, all the time.

Monday

Dearest,

A <u>very</u> good time was had by all last night! After I finished writing you, Bobbie and I undressed and prepared for bed. When I opened the door into the back bedroom where the 3 rats were, you would have thought it as an old man's convention – all three were snoring! Bobbie and I had convulsions! Well, they slept until Susan cried out (dreaming) about 4:30. Woke Dianne and she woke Carol. Then the fun started. I took Carol into the living room and laid down on the couch with her. She fell asleep just after Theo's alarm clock went off. When she heard it, she sat up and said "Wotyat?" I gently laid her down and told her to listen. Her little eyes closed and we both went to sleep. She woke up about 8:00 and so did Dianne. I fixed their breakfast and while Bobbie and Susan still slept, I washed Theo's breakfast dishes and ours, then washed Bobbie's clothes and started Susan's oatmeal and Bobbie's Café-au-lait. She slept until 10:00 and Susan slept until 10:30! After they ate and I had my second cup of coffee, we made beds and Lily invited us down for coffee and cinnamon toast. By the time, we got back it was Carol's lunch time so I fed her and put her to bed. We ate and in walks Daddy and Mama with the best news outside of your coming home! Daddy has a passenger run out of here to Lafayette! What we've all been dreaming of and praying for the seven years he's been in T (*Texas*). More he'll live here and just lay over in Lafayette. Isn't that great news! Naturally, we all were a little delirious about all afternoon. We all had beans and biscuits, fresh garden snap beans, baked chicken and lots of everything. I would have been awfully happy except for one thing – It's been a week since I received a card from you and about a week and a half since a letter. I don't want to dwell on it, sweet, but letters surely do help this homesick feeling. I may be with loved ones in my old home, but I can bet I'm just as lonesome for you as you are for us! Maybe the mailman will have something for me tomorrow. I hope!

We've been having high winds and rain here for the past three days. It acts just like it did before that hurricane last year. I'll bet there's a storm somewhere. The Mississippi is on a terrific rise. The greatest in 100 years! Wouldn't that be something now – what with the war and all.

Of course, Theo doesn't know anymore of his status. Dorothy has bad word frequently from Van and he has your address so I hope he writes. If you want his, I'll send it.

David P. taken by Esther Jennings – 1938 Ikes

Bottom left: Sarah Ann "Daid" Mouton Quattlebaum, Baby Ann's mother, with an unidentified child, April 1938.
Right: Daid, as a young woman, c. 1917.

This is about all for tonight, sweetheart, so I guess I'd better close this as it's 10:30 and I could stand a little shut-eye. We just got back from taking Daddy to the round house for his first run! Swell huh!

I love you forever,

Your Mommy

May 3, 1944 – from Missouri Ave, Houston, to Camp Lee, VA

Tuesday p.m.
May 2, 1944

Dearest One,

I'm just about at the end of my rope. That's why I sent that telegram. If you're in the hospital, I won't be surprised because I think that's the only reason you wouldn't write – you could never be too busy to write your mommy – would you? Golly! I hope not anyway.

Well, I'll know tomorrow.

I'm going to go to Newgulf next week I guess. I'm going to Bobbie's tomorrow to spend the day, but I'm not leaving here until I finish this telegram business I started. If I don't get an answer by the time the mail man gets here with no letter again – fur is really going to start flying!

Midnight – bong!

Betsy asked me to go to the show with her and I just got back. I feel a great deal better about the whole thing. We saw "Upstairs in Mabel's Room". Don't miss it – it'll make you want to live in marital bliss (?) again! You'll understand the question mark when you see the picture.

This isn't going to be one of my usual lengthy epistles. I'm going to cut short now and pray for an answer to my telegram and an answer to a few of my questions – a letter wouldn't be hard to take either. I know you're busy, but a card now and then would sure help morale on the home front. Brother, if you think you're having a tough time rehabilitating, just remember you're not the only one. A letter means a great deal to you, as you've told me, well, you're not the only one.

Forgive this letter – hope my attitude is different with a new day. Remember I love you all my life, and I'll go on loving you until the last leaf shrivels up and peeps out on the dear old world.

Bye now, sweet –

I love you.

Yours forever,

Mommy

May 5, 1944 – from Missouri Ave, Houston, to Camp Lee, VA

Inside envelope, Ann writes – Put both arms around yourself and give my Popsy a big hug – make like its from his Mommy.

Thursday p.m.

Hello Sweet,

Well, the radio is playing "I'll Get by" and if you remember the words – as long as I have you "you'll know how I feel!" However, at this moment I'm not so sure I have you. You see, your wire said you'd dispatched an Air Mail Monday. Tomorrow is Friday and if I get it then, that's five days and Martha Lee gets A.M. from England in six and seven days! Some mail svc we have here in the dear old U.S.! (I'm kidding, I only hope I'll never have to wait for mail from overseas.)

Speaking of Mart – she had a letter from John day before yesterday. He took his examination for that Randolph Field job and had 105 degree fever! They sent him to the hospital and that's where he wrote from. He didn't say what it was or anything. If it were the other way around, if we here at home had written something like that without any other word, the cables would really have burnt up. That's the way you soldiers do us – you don't think we're going through anything, but, brother, that mental anguish can be worse than the actual suffering – but I can't tell <u>you</u> that, you found that out when our little squirt made her debut! That's another reason I worried about not hearing from you. I hope the telegram didn't make you mad and I hope that I haven't written anything that's hurt you because I love you so much, it would hurt me to know that I did, however I was so hurt at first when I didn't hear from you (no letter since April 20th) – (a card on the 20th, but not a letter since the 10th!) Almost a month! Anyway, after the first hurt was over, I started to get worried, then when the third week started rolling by, I could see you being shipped overseas, or in the hospital and all sorts of other silly things like the first I mentioned.

I don't have a thing to say so I guess I'd better close. I hope I have a letter tomorrow – then I'll start blabbing again. I wrote a 6 page letter last night after the telegram – what will I write you after a letter – wow!

I adore you –

Love,

Baby

May 6, 1944 – from Missouri Ave, Houston, to Camp Lee, VA

Inside envelope, Ann writes: Does this letter make up for the short one I wrote last night? I adore you, you lug!

Friday p.m., May 5

My dearest,

It was so swell to hear from you I hardly know what to say. All I can I guess is just say I now know what's going in and I promise not to get upset again like that.

It made me feel almost as good as if I'd seen you and you can imagine how good that is!

I talked to Betsy tonight. She received a letter from Mac inquiring about you. I was so glad I'd received your letter because now I know myself. He said to tell you hello for him. Betty said it was swell of you to think of them. I don't know their address offhand, but if you send it to the office – c/o E.E. Stone Lumber Co. – they'll be sure to get it.

I received the bank statement today and our balance is really looking sad! Your check was for $5.00 and it was in there. I'm going to put it on my stub so I can check it off. You don't have to keep a record of it. Whenever you write a check just list them for me and I'll put them on my stub. It'll be easier for both of us that way. $326.54 is the balance and I put $35.00 in the savings account. I wouldn't have done it had I known I wouldn't receive my allotment or money from I.B.M. before now. Honey, I have all of your S.O. slips and the slips you receive with your paychecks and I don't know how to explain the adj. salary check of 20 and some add dollars you asked about. Do you want me to send the slip that was with it? That doesn't tell anymore about it than I did. I'm going to call Peggy in the morning to find out when our payments start and I'll ask her about that, too. The way Johnny explained it the day he called to tell you when they paid that overtime in July and dated it wrong that you asked him to find out about, he said they paid you too much that last week (you worked just 'til Wednesday and got paid 'til Saturday, didn't you? Could that be the reason for a deduction? And maybe that was the first 1/3 salary check I'm supposed to be getting – huh? I'll find out tomorrow I just happened to think of that. Hope you understand what I'm trying to say – I just read it over and I'm beginning to wonder just what I mean! Heh, heh, same old gal!

Oh, golly when you spoke of that furlough! Do you think at any time you'll be able to have a visit from your wife and child. I don't mean particularly at Camp Lee, but speaking of the duration in general – wouldn't that be something – Really honey, I'm scared to think about such things too much because it just make me all the more miserable.

It seems the past few letters I've written I've either hoped you get one or something before the one I wrote the night before arrives. Well, here I am hoping again! I just couldn't write a jolly letter last night, I felt too bad. I'm OK today tho, my husband hasn't forgotten me, he still loves me, in fact in view of the aforementioned letter, I really think he adores me and his little family and misses us as much as we miss him, wot say?

Oh yes – I wanted to tell you about John. Martha Lee received a letter from him yesterday. He said he had lost consciousness after they called the ambulance for him and the next thing he knew, he was in a hospital bed with 25 other boys in the same room and he had his eye all bandaged up! He said he had an idea he had been operated on but for what he doesn't know. Someone else, probably the nurse, wrote the letter for him and it really sounded funny. He also said he called the nurse and was so neglected he had to prescribe for himself. He really raised hell. You see he wasn't in his hospital so he threatened to get up and go there if something wasn't done. He said he knew he was dying and they gave him Pennessalin (that new drug). He called for it and told them how to administer it. He said he wanted Mart to tell the family and to tell the world that that was the grandest stuff known of. He said after he had it, it took him just about two hours to snap out of it. It really saved his life. It was a very pessimistic letter and you know how optimistic he usually is. It really hurt Mart to read it because she knew how sick he must be. I imagine just as soon as he's able they'll ship him home.

Gladys and Leon Lampe came in this morning. They said they were so sorry they couldn't have gotten to see you in S.A. and I'm sorry that this letter brings so much sad news but I must tell you some news they brought with them. Cousin Myra is very sick and they think she is dying. I think Mama is going back with them. The funny part of it is Memere, her closest friend, died of the same thing. Mama is pretty upset about it.

Well, I guess the best news I can give you now is about our little chick. She is precious and you know about the surprise by the time you get this letter so will say no more about it. This afternoon she was the cutest I've ever seen her. She took your letter and climbed up on the couch and opened it and began to read it! She started off with DaDa say – and that's all I could understand! I wish you could hear her talk. Cutest thing!

I'm going to have the brakes checked. I also want to see if the wheels need aligning because when you step on the brake it goes way over to the left. Other than that, tho, the little buggy's in perfect shape. Do you know what you want to do with it yet?

I'm enclosing something I think you'll get a big kick out of (I only wish I could enclose myself!) (and the chick, of course!) I'm going now. I could write on and on but if I did I wouldn't have anything to tell you tomorrow nite. Say, that K.P. must be awful. I told Louise and she said to tell you she said hello and that she was praying for you. I am too, sweet. I'm glad you had your eyes checked, but it was the underside of the lids I was speaking of. – Sunday, April 30 – I dreamed I was with you and we weren't at home, it seemed like we were on clouds – and a little cloud by the side held the baby and her crib. You and I were just like at 1713. I love you so much! What did you dream that night? I'm trying to get all of this on three pages so I can send it A.M. By the way, did you know that the A.M. (Air Mail) I received today (you wrote it Sunday night) was postmarked Camp Lee, May 4, 10a.m. – that was yesterday morning and I got it today. Did it lay around over there or did you forget to mail it? Bye now. I love you all my life and looking forward to another letter.

Yours, Mommy

(Note: Starting "Sunday, April 30..." in the last paragraph, Ann began writing very small to ensure she didn't use up more paper!)

May 7, 1944 – from Missouri Ave, Houston, to Camp Lee, VA

Inside envelope, Ann writes: To one from the other used-to-be-inhabitants of Seventh Heaven, namely 1713.

Saturday p.m.,
May 6, 1944

Hello Sweetheart,

How's my boy this evening? Hope fine. I am and so is the baby. I do feel a little foolish now sure 'nuff since I received a letter from you again today postmarked April 27. I guess the mail is held up at Camp Lee, and I want you to put the day and date on each letter so I can tell what's happening. Funny isn't it? Are you getting my letters in succession or how? I know the Air Mail's beat the regular mail but just how long does it take? The letter I received yesterday (the day was Sunday on the top of your first page) was postmarked May 4 – and I got it May 5. It would be swell if true – what say?

Theo and Bobbie and the two kids were over for their usual Saturday afternoon play period. I let Theo use your Zippo lighter. I found it in the drawer when I straightened our papers out. So, if you can't find the lighter at the P.X., you can forget it, that is unless you've started smoking again and want it. Do you ever smoke your pipe? I like to picture you smoking it. You know how much I love to see you with a pipe in your mouth.

Sweet, I believe I'm going to take the baby to an allergist. I want your opinion on it, but this hit and miss proposition is about to get me down. Her throat cleared up when I took her off of milk but she broke out on her face, arms, and the front of her legs today. The backs of her legs are still broken out but they seem to be more so today. The only thing I can think of is lamb. I gave her a lamb chop at noon today and she hasn't had one in quite awhile – however, she didn't seem to have any extra trouble when last she ate some. I just think it might be better for a few days of needle sticking than months, years of scratching and itching – Maybe, it's just a few things and then maybe it's just one thing. I want you to think about it and let me know. Of course, Dr. Balyeat in Okla. City is out because if I get that far away from home, I'm just afraid I'd just keep on going until I found myself in your arms. There are some good doctors here, but if you want it any other way, I'll do what you think best. Dr. Wallis is just swell but I just can't seem to think he knows any more about it than we do.

I don't know whether I told you or not but I put our bonds in a safe deposit box with Aunt Tennie's.

George Harvey (Garland's husband) has been drafted and their baby is due in about a week! Isn't that awful? He hasn't received his notice when to leave yet, but they're hoping the baby arrives before he's sent.

Speaking of babies, I asked you one day how you would like to hear I was p.g. too. You said you knew in what condition I was when you left and you expect me to be when you get back – well, my friend (don't get me wrong, I'm not!), you know you left here after I menstruated and how do you know I have since you're away! Just answer that please! Oh, golly, I wish we were together so we could make arguments like we used to. It was so much fun, wasn't it – kidding each other! No, sweet, as long as we both have breaths in our bodies, I'll belong entirely to you and you'll belong to me. That's poetry, isn't it? Sounds like it and I really believe our life together is like poetry – don't you – it's beautiful enough to be anyway.

I'd better stop thinking, or, like you – will go over the hill.

Baby Ann's parents, Daid and Bob Quattlebaum, in 1917, just before Bob went to France to serve in World War I. Daid is pregnant with their first daughter, Effie Roberta "Bobbie" at the time.

Daddy and Mama and I are down here in the sun room. They're reading. Gladys, Leon and Aunt Tennie have gone to bed. They really are early birds. They go to bed with the chickens and get up with them. They have coffee with Aunt Tennie and then they have breakfast and by the time we get up, Gladys comes up when Mama gets up and starts making beds. M feels funny about it and starts to help her. You know M at 8 am.! You can imagine Mama making a bed before having her coffee – puts her in a horrible mood! Oh gee – it's really good! But she's in marvelous spirits since Daddy's come home. We all are, but I guess I'm kinda nervous because you can't have everything. Are you nervous? I guess our happiness and complete life ruined us, or at least it did me. I'm trying hard, honey, I really am, but you can't be at peace when you're unhappy. I guess it's the same way with you.

The mixer motor is finally ready. I'm going to get it Monday. I'm also going to make some fudge for you because I have the condensed milk. I'm going to make cookies though, I promise!

Just send the shorts back. I got them at Shudde's and I know they'll fix you up right.

Aunt Hattie is better, thank goodness, and I think the Williams' are all better for it. A thing like that upsets the whole household.

Well, sweet, I think I'm going to close this. It's too thick to send Air Mail, so will just send it regular.

Oh, yes, I wanted to tell you – or rather ask you if you knew a Mr. Reed down at the office. I don't know anything about him except he came here just about the time you left. I talked to Peggy today and she told me he had died of a heart attack. He was about 50 years old, but it was a great shock to all. She said she (Peggy) isn't pregnant, but Leonard's working like the devil (I mean down at the office – that sounded funny, didn't it?) I could go on writing all night but will stop so I won't grow boring. Bye now, sleep tight, don't let the bed bugs bite (I won't, not unless they bite you first) – I love you all my life and both your girls miss hell out of you (miss hell in you too). Be always as you are now – I love you,

Your Mommy

---

*May 7, 1944 – **from Bill** in Camp Lee, Virginia*

Sunday 5/7/44

My sweet little wife and baby,

Well, here it is Sunday again. Four weeks of basic is finished and two more to go. Then I start technical. This week I go on the firing range for three days. All the rifle practice I have had so far has been practicing "dry" firing. Can you imagine shooting a rifle without ammunition? Well that's exactly what I have been doing for the past three weeks with the exception of five shots fired with real ammunition. I think I told you that I was going to tell you what my score was. Well my score was 22 out of a possible 25 – two bulls eyes and 3 next to the bulls eye.

(Bill included a drawing of his shots on a target with the two bulls eyes and 3 just below the bull eyes. He added a caption, "The dots show where I hit the target. Bulls eye counts five.")

This target is fired at 200 yds with the U.S. Army Springfield 1903 rifle. (Theo will probably know what kind of rifle this is.) We leave early tomorrow morning for the range. I have heard some talk about us going out and staying all three days without coming back at nite, but I think we will return every evening. As I understand, we will do practice firing the first two days and then the third day we fire for record. If I qualify for sharpshooter, I get to fire the Carbine. The Carbine is really a sweet little rifle. It weighs only 5 1/4 lbs, is 35 1/4 long and is semi-automatic and will fire 15 rounds of ammunition without reloading. So much for rifle marksmanship anyway. I'm going to try for at least a sharpshooter. Expert is the highest.

Sweetheart, I don't believe I have told you anything of the country around here – almost anywhere you go there are piney woods. They are really beautiful. Trees everywhere. Our training area is located right among the pine trees. Our lecture classes are held in open top tents which are also among the pine trees. To give you a better picture of our classroom, just imagine a whole platoon of men seated together on benches right on the base ground in the middle of a pine forest. In front of the men, stands a 2nd Lieutenant on a platform. To help him with the lecture, the Lt. has charts and equipment of various kinds depending on what the lecture is about. All this is encircled by tenting canvass. No top on it. You can just look up and see the sky and pine branches above you. Do you get the picture? When the lecture is finished, we go out and practice what has been lectured.

I just got back from a little meeting (6:00pm). The meeting was about us going to the firing range tomorrow. We get up at 4:30 in the morning, eat breakfast, clean the barracks and leave at 5:30. We were assigned to our details and firing order while on the range for the three days. My detail is working in the pits operating the targets. This is my detail for all three mornings. I do my firing in the afternoons of the three days. Pardon me while I toot my whistle again. What I mean is from all the hard work I did on the practice range for the past three weeks, I hope to get a pretty good score.

Now I'll go to a little different subject. I went over the landing net for the first time last Thursday. I'm sure you know what the landing net is. You have seen them in picture shows. They are the nets that hang over the side of ships and soldiers scramble over them. The first two times we were scheduled to go over the net, I was on some detail and I missed it. The first two times, the boys went over without any equipment but last week went over with full field equipment less the rifle. Sometime later, we go over with full field equipment including the rifle. Some stuff. The net is 40 ft high and hangs perpendicular to the ground.

Sweetheart, I hope you received the air mail letters I sent you. All together so far I have sent you 3 air mails not including this one. Let me know if you received them. In your letter I received yesterday (Sat), you said you had received my telegram but from the way I understood, you had not received the letters. I'm sure I am receiving all your letters because I receive one almost every day. When I do miss a day, I receive two the next. Keep up the good work, and I promise to do better myself.

Well, my sweet, I think I had better close now and hit the hay because I have to get up at 4:30 in the morn.

I have looked high and low for the Williams' address but could not find it. I'm sure you didn't send it because I went through all your letters and picked out the address you gave me and put them in my address book and theirs wasn't there. So send it to me. I want to drop them a line. I know it's on Leak Street but don't know the number.

Tell everyone hello for me. Kiss yourself and my daughter for me.

I love you all my life, and I do miss you.

Love and Kisses,

Bill

May 8, 1944 – from Missouri Ave, Houston, to Camp Lee, VA

Inside the envelope, Ann writes: How I'd love to take you in my arms, and – well, you think of the rest.

Sunday p.m.
May 7, 1944

Dearest,

Another Sunday and just about the same, except I kept the kids so Bobbie and Theo could go to the show. They went to the Tower – "Guadalcanal Diary". When they returned I asked each how they like it. Theo said it was alright (as per usual!) and Bobbie shuddered and said "Gruesome". That was that!

Carol ate a big supper at 5:30. Then when we ate (just before she went to bed), I put her in the high chair and gave her a chicken bone with a little chicken on it. She just started with that one! When I took it away from her, she begged for another and by the time I took her up for bed, she had finished two legs and a thigh! Sweet little thing – she had your picture out today and showing everybody her "Da-da!" I have that small picture of you in my billfold and she begs for the billfold every time I pick up my purse. I do wish you could have a larger one made in your uniform. I'd really like a billfold size one, if you can't get a regular portrait made. Honey, I'd sure like to have one in your cup. I'd love to see you – period! Cause, I love you – see!

Say, honey, next Sunday's Mother's Day and I don't want you to forget your Mother. I'm going to send her something, but she'd sure like to get a little something from you.

Leon and Gladys and Mama are leaving in the morning. Leon just said to tell you hello and hopes you'll be here the next time they come. He said he wished you lots of luck.

Another thing that's been pretty swell happened today. Emile finished his land training and is going to sea (just for training) and got a furlough. He's on his way to Lafayette now. Came through here this afternoon and we got to see him. He's sunburned like the devil but just looks swell. I only wish my honey could have called me from the station. (You'd better let me know – you so and so – so I can look like your dreams.)

I'm going to meet Earline Orr, Mildred Buchanan - and I think another girl – up town tomorrow to get the gifts and prizes for our party Thursday night. I'll tell you all about it tomorrow night. I'm rather out of conversation tonight. I can't seem to think of anything to gab about so I guess I'd better go while you still love me.

Hope I get another letter tomorrow but if I don't, I'll understand! I love you all my life and forgive me for this short letter. Bye now.

Love you just oodles,

Yours forever,

Mommy

May 9, 1944 – from Missouri Ave, Houston to Camp Lee, VA

Inside the envelope , Ann writes: Lucy's lonesome for Johnny. Tell him when you see him.

Monday p.m.

Dearest One,

I have more news for you today. I'll begin with the dawn and bring the day to a close. It began rather early as Mama left for San Antonio with Gladys and Leon about 6 a.m. Then Daddy was called so they took Daddy and Aunt Tennie to work then went on their way. The baby woke a little after seven and after we breakfasted, we dressed and after the house was straight, we went out to Bobbie's. That was about 9:30 when we arrived Bobbie and Lily were washing clothes. We had coffee when they finished and fooled around until lunch. I put Carol to bed and had a sandwich and watched Susan and Dianne and Jerry while Bobbie and Lily went to the grocery store. Then, when they came back, I went to town and met Earline Orr, Margarite Evans, and Mildred Buchanan. We walked from 2 to 5 and I really wish I had your G.I. shoes with the special built-up arches in them! Oh boy, do my puppies howl right now!

I got back to Bobbie's about 5:35 and found that she had taken the kids to a birthday party three houses down. Dianne was perfect but Susan had a fight with a little boy and Carol was just wonderful. Bobbie said she played with all the children but when Susan started crying, Dianne did too, so you can imagine what happened! Carol pucked all up and started that sobbing of hers. A Mrs. Titsworth who was there almost cried herself! When Bobbie mentioned the name, I asked her if she was young. She said yes, but she had a little boy about 6 yrs. old. Doesn't that sound like your friend? What were their first names? I wish you'd find out. I mean let me know and I'll find out more. Bobbie said she'd try to find out for me. I'm sure if I heard her name (or his), I'd recognize it. Anyway, we had supper (chow to you, my G.I. Joe) and left there at 5 min to eight. The sweet little thing was so tired she could barely talk. But she stood up in the car next to me all the way home showing me the "lights". She looked precious today. Had on her white dotted swiss dress with bonnet to match. She looked like a big doll!

You've received several letters from Vice Presidents of the company. Do you want me to send them to you or would you rather me save them and put them where you can keep them? Even one from T.G. himself! By the way, I received a check from IBM today for $73.87 from March 16 to April 30. That makes my monthly allowance $48.75. Do you want me to put this check in savings or just put it in our checking? I'd like to put it away for with only $2.00 I could get a $100 war bond. However, I

Bill, Theo, (unidentified man), and Bob with Dianne, Susan and Carol, c. 1944.

haven't received any allotment from your present employer yet. Hope that turns up before long! Let me know right away though, so I won't have to keep the check too long.

But getting back to the day – after I put Carol to bed, I went down to Granny's. She received a letter from Wesley and he's at the Anzio beachhead in Italy. He said it's been pretty hot over there and he's not talking of the weather! He's been in the Tanks Corps but has just been transferred to the Q.M. Corps. He said to tell us hello and to tell me that the Army got one swell soldier when they drafted you. I'm going to write him tomorrow. Granny is sending his letter to Doris so you will get to read the latest one.

Before I close I want to ask you if you want Theo's radio. He said he'd have it fixed and sent to you if you did. He's crazy about your lighter and really shows off with it. I hope you didn't mind my letting him use it. It was just laying in the drawer. I would have liked it but I'm glad I did it cause he gave me 3 gas coupons today and told me to be sure and ask you about the radio – so I know he appreciates it.

Well, sweet, I'll go now so I can send this Air Mail. I haven't really finished telling you all about everything as I promised but if I did I'd have to send it by ox-cart and hire it at that. Be sweet and write soon. I love you all my life and miss you more and more each day.

I'll be loving you always,

Mommy

May 10, 1944 – from Missouri Ave, Houston, to Camp Lee, VA

I am not sure who Ann is referring to when she talks about Granny and Pop-Pop in the following letter. The only grandparents that are still living at this time are not called Granny and Pop-Pop. They may be friends of the family.

Tuesday

Hello Sweetheart,

I'll continue with last night's letter – rather where I left off with last night's. I wanted to tell you I'd received all your letters to date including the one you wrote Sunday. Got it today and the mail service is getting pretty good, eh? I'm so glad you're well and it's swell about your teeth. I'm also happy to hear something is being done about your back. I never did think anything of your knees, but maybe all the exercise is making it sore. Hope your back isn't hurting you more than you're telling me. But I'm sure it doesn't because we decided Honesty is the best policy and I know that's best. It keeps either one from worrying.

Oh, gee, I sure got off the track. I wanted to tell you how proud I am of your score on the rifle range. Hope you make your marksmanship and maybe even expert! I know you're shooting for that anyway! I love you, mess-pot!

George just called and said he has a 7-pound baby girl – Garland is fine. I'm glad that's over. I was sorta worried about her. She had gained 48 pounds and that ain't funny.

Anyway, what I was going to say – your letter describing your health and beautiful body gave me a funny little thrill when I read it so I thought I'd describe your two girls to you and maybe you'd get a thrill – so here goes –

Your daughter is about 1 inch shorter than Susan and wears the same size shoe! Her hair is long now and still wears it in bangs. She has her beautiful blue eyes still bright and has an adorable laugh. When she laughs, it sounds like silver over a waterfall! Her eyes are very expressive and has plenty of devil in them. She's loud as all get out, too. She's really precious. I have her in pinafores as you'll see in her colored pictures you'll get in about 6 weeks. Hope they're as good as the negatives look. Anyway, you have a very lovely daughter. As for her other developments, she has a precious way of talking. Says quite a few things and asks for you every day. Tonight, she asked for "Momo" and I told her where she was. Evidently "San Antonio" was associated with you and she started in on "I want my Da-Da" – I'm OK until she starts that! Don't you think you have a big girl?

Now for your wife. Your daughter is brilliant, but I'm afraid this may be dull so hold your hat (?), and here goes. –

I weigh 107 – wonderful, isn't it? I took up two more of my last summer dressed today. I've made two dresses, the green and blue ones I drew for you – the green one is (*Ann drew small picture of dress*) – and the blue one is (*Ann drew another dress, and labeled it "woo-woo!"*) Hope you like them. I have two new blouses to wear with my suit (it's a honey, my suit is). One blouse is all colored flowers on a white background and looks like this (*Ann drew a blouse*), and the other is blue and white striped (*Ann drew another blouse*). I want to have my picture taken in my suit with the colored (the first one) blouse so you can see how your thin wife looks now. My hair is real long – down to my shoulders and am thinking of cutting it. How about it? I have some patent (brown) shoes but the bags to match are $10.00 plus tax so I'm waiting until the dear old war is over. I'm going to make a hat cause on $80.00 bucks a month, I'll have to! Here I was going to describe myself but am on clothes. I do miss talking over my clothes with you. I never realized how much I depended on you for little things until now. I knew the big things but not things like talking over movies and whether I ought to have my hair cut or not. Gee, I guess you haven't had much time to think of those things yet. It's good that you're as busy as you are. I'd love to be with you since you described the scenery. You know how I like scenery (I wonder if my husband and I will notice any scenery when we see each other!) Granny and I went to town this morning. I drove her down to get her hair cut. She said it would be swell if we could drive up. I'd drive her and Pop-Pop. I shut my ears real quick so I wouldn't be tempted (it wouldn't take much!)

I'm going to quit now so hope I've written something you like to hear. My arms are still the same length – they'll just about get around your neck, if we stand real close together – Sleep tight and dream of your little family – I love you all my life and think of you every minute of the day.

I love you terrifically,

Your Mommy

P.S.: Have you noticed the flaps?

May 11, 1944 – from Missouri Ave, Houston, to Camp Lee, VA

Wednesday

Hello sweet,

This is going to be short as its pretty late and I want to roll up my hair for the party tomorrow night. We cleaned up today and put up the curtains in the sun room. When Louise and I were stretching them I couldn't help but think – we're just one more day closer to stretching our own curtains for our "home" (no matter how humble) someday.

I took Pop-Pop to church about 6:00 and after I bathed and put the chick to bed, I went back for him (about 8:00) and we drove out South Main and had frozen custard. Those poor old souls are so lonesome for Doris it's just pitiful. If I get the chance – it won't be tomorrow – I want to write her. I also owe Max, Ore Nell, and Sis letters – hope I can get that done by Friday anyway.

I cleaned up the sun room and started in on the dining room. Carol is scared to death of the vacuum and talks all the time it's being used to hide her fright. Anyway, I heard a peculiar silence and came into the sun room to investigate. Our child was sitting up on the couch with the big ash tray which I'd used as a waste basket for all the rest of the ash trays and was calmly eating cigarette butts! Her dress (the pretty little blue one your Mother bought for her the last time we were there together) which I had put on her especially for "dress-up" ~~ocassion occasion occasion, oh darn! — how about a spelling lesson? How do you spell it, anyway? - Back to the doings of your daughter — Her dress was filthy, her hands and face looked like she'd spent the night in a coal gin, and she laughed when I caught her. I cleaned off the couch — which was the dirtiest thing I've ever seen! I couldn't whip her though — she looked too cute — grinning up at me like that. Well, after I took off her dress (she had on pants, a slip and shoes), she came walking into the kitchen where I was disassembling the vacuum (sp?) and handed me her slip — torn to shreds! Well, I fussed at her but she really looked precious, that fat little thing in silk panties! Then after I put up the vacuum, she came walking into the living room — sans panties! I really threw a spell! That was undoubtedly the sweetest thing I've seen since I took my eyes off you last!~~

~~That's about the crop as far as the news of the day is concerned. I'm sitting here just hating the idea of the rolling up of the hair business but it must be done — so bye now and write soon. Love you oodles and oodles — Keep yourself well and don't do anything I wouldn't do.~~

~~Bye now~~
~~Sleep tight, etc. —~~
~~I love you all my life,~~

~~Your Mommy~~

May 11, 1944 – from Newgulf, TX, to Camp Lee, VA - From Matilda "Tillie" Genzer, Bill's mother, in Newgulf

A greeting card, on front says "In the Service" – with Love to Our Boy on Mother's Day
Inside card – On Mother's Day, we think of you, And though we miss you more than ever, We three are bound by ties of love, Dear Son, which distance cannot sever! Mom and Pop

Letter included:

Dear Son,

I really was glad when I got that Mother's Day card and letter yesterday and thank you very much. But didn't get the picture you said you sent yet, but I guess it will be here today or tomorrow. You just don't know how glad all of us were when Pop came home from work yesterday and said got a letter from Bill. All three of us was reading it at one time. If you can, do write at least once a week.

I am glad you are getting along fine.

I am really proud of my Son, Daughter-in-Law and baby too. Got a letter from them the other day saying they were just fine and that they will be coming over for a while soon. We will go after them as soon as she let us know.

We are getting along just fine.

I think Pop will take his vacation soon, just when I don't know.

James Armstrong said he was coming to see you but he had to leave again, but he said he was going to write you, did you get a letter from him. I think Sis sent him your address.

He said he wasn't but about 2 ½ hours from there where he was, until where you are.

Well Sis won't have but one more week of school and now the parties will start and on the 26th graduation will be.

I am sorry the cake was all broken up but I guess it couldn't be helped. We will send you another package in a few days.

Well, I think I must go now and get this mailed. You be good and write. Sis will be writing you tonight she has quit a bit on her hands now these last days of school.

Much Love from us all,

Mom, Pop and Sis

May 13, 1944 – from Missouri Ave, Houston, TX, to Camp Lee, VA

Friday a.m.

Hello sweet,

Just a word or two to say I'll write and tell you all about the party last night in my letter tonite. I have some news about the IBM family and its relatives and a few other things to tell you. I didn't get in until after midnite so I didn't write. But here's the Thursday letter anyway.

We're fine and everything's hunky dory. Missed you last night. Will tell all tonight.

Love you always,

Your own,

Baby

May 13, 1944 – from Missouri Ave, Houston, TX, to Camp Lee, VA

Friday p.m.

Hello sweet,

The short note I wrote this morning is still sitting on the buffet but it will get mailed with this one in the morning. I was too sleepy to write last night, but couldn't let you miss that "letter a day" for anything!

I had a pretty hectic day yesterday. It started at 7:30 and ended about 1 p.m. I guess you laugh at the hour we arise in the a.m., but you know me! The baby sleeps now until 7:30 or 8:00. Her usual time is a quarter to eight. I put her to bed at 8:00p.m., starting around 7:30. I usually start with the bath and stuff and by 8:00 she's usually all tucked in. She was precious tonight in the tub. She put the rag on the bottom of the tub, smoothed it out and usually when she does that with a handkerchief or blanket she slaps it down. Well, she tried it in the tub and splashed it all over her face – rag, water and all! She nearly died laughing. I had to dry her eyes and hair, too! I'll tell you something more about her later.

Right now, I want to tell you about the party last night. It was pretty good but would have been much better if this hadn't happened. I wanted to cry when I laid eyes on Pauline Connelley. Honey, I was never so shocked in my life. You know she has arthritis, well, she used to weigh 110, if that much. If she does, her legs weigh the extra 10. They're quite large but her arms and body are as small as Bobbie's. I felt so awful when I saw her I said I'd never gripe again, however I've been in a pretty low mood all day. Something happened today, tho, that really made me feel swell. More about that later.

Sweetheart, Frankie told me that Willie had had her baby about a month ago and it lived about 5 days. He had a real big head and no skin on his legs. Willie told her that it hurt her to lose her baby but since it was deformed, she'd rather have it that way. I guess that's another reason I've had the R.A.'s today. This is an awful bearer of awful news but I've saved the best for the last.

Have you heard the new Draft Law? Men in the age bracket 26 to 29, employed in essential war work are to be deferred. Men from 30 to 37 are to be deferred if employed in anything. That'll take care of the deadbeats. Doesn't that make you sick? Well, even if it came too late for us maybe Theo will be able to stay at home.

I'm going out there tomorrow night to stay with the kids while they go to Lily's surprise birthday party for Bruce so I expect to be able to catch up on my correspondence then. I wrote Sis today. I imagine I'll go down next weekend.

Well, now, for that happy last moment I've been speaking of.

We received the pictures and oh golly I want to see you so bad. It's a grand picture and you should have seen your baby! She nearly had a fit! She took mine and tried to tear it out of the frame. I think she was thinking you'd step out if she released you! She showed it to everybody! We're both so proud! Mother was really tickled. She said it was just like you to remember her. When she showed it to Louise, she wanted to know what you'd sent her and then she laughed. She was so glad you'd sent something. I didn't expect anything. I thought you'd either write, or send a card, or I was even hoping for flowers, but I didn't have any idea this would be it. I'm really thrilled with it. Thanks, sweet. Hope you'll like ours. I want to have a regular portrait made. Would you like one of Carol and one of me, or one of us together? That's what I had in mind, one of us together, but if you have a better idea, let me know. Answer this and the radio questions. Theo wants to know cause if you're going to be there another 8 weeks, you may want it. I'm going to quit now. I'll tell you more tomorrow night. Thanks again for the pictures, sweet, the little one is for my billfold and my heart. I love you all my life and we miss you.
Kisses from,

Your two girls

May 15, 1944 – from Missouri Ave, Houston, TX, to Camp Lee, VA

Sunday (*written on "United Nations Victorious" stationery*)

Hello sweetheart,

This is my Saturday night letter, too, because I came out to Bobbie's yesterday and after I put the baby to bed, I found out the stationery was in the drawer of the chest of drawers in that room. I'll draw a diagram of how we did it. (*Diagram shows Front Bedroom with a box, door left high, then, left to right, "big bed", "crib", then "chest of drawers", with French doors on the right wall in the center.*) So you can see it was impossible to get it. I had plenty of time to write and I really missed it too. I was just dying to tell you about the lapel locket you sent. Honey, I love it. I wanted to put the picture of you in your uniform (the little one), but it was too big. Maybe a snapshot in your uniform will do it.

Baby Ann's mother, Daid, known as Momo to her grandchildren and great-grandchildren, with granddaughter Dianne, in front of their home at 1203 Missouri Ave, Houston, Texas, c. 1942.

Anyway, I want to put Carol's picture in the other side. I'm so proud of it. I've had it on since I got it. It came in the early mail Saturday and here was one surprised human being. I thought the pictures were my Mother's Day gift, so you can imagine what happened when Louise brought it up. I was shaking like a leaf! I've never been so pleasantly surprised in my life except the day you walked in after you left for the Army! Thanks sweet, hope I can do something like that for you someday.

Well, now I'll tell you about the party last night. The party started about 9:15, at least that's when B and I left. About 10:00, here came Bruce and Johnny and made me go down for a drink. Bruce stayed here and I went down and had a drink. Then came on back. Then about 12:00, Theo came and I went down for another. Bobbie and two of the girls came down about 12:30 and Bobbie was sick as a horse (you know B!) Theo stayed until about 2:00. Then came home. I didn't sleep, even though I was in bed with B until Theo came home. He was quite full himself, although he didn't get sick. A fine time was had by all! Including me when Carol woke up at 6:00a.m. (she's training herself at nite!) and after she wee'd, I put her in bed with B and me. She was quiet until a little after seven so I got up and fed her. Dianne followed at 8, Susan at 9:00 and B at 10:30 with Theo about the same. We went over to Mama's and had dinner and spent the early part of the afternoon. Then we straightened of the house when we got here. I'm going in to get cool and comfortable in a little bit because we're expecting Mama, Daddy, and Aunt Tennie out here in a few minutes. I'll write more later.

Well – here it is about 9:00. The kids are all bathed, abed, and asleep. Sweet little Carol is really tired tonight. The funniest thing happened today when we were over at Mother's. Dianne had about three pieces of candy. She turned around and one piece was gone. She made Susan open her mouth and she had one in her mouth. Mama said she had given her one and that was it. Well, later Carol came walking into the front room with candy all over her mouth. When the little episode above occurred, she was standing right by Dianne and had her arms, fists clenched, behind her back – you know how she stands. Well, the little chicken had the candy in her fist while she was peering down Susan's throat with Dianne! That's terrible, but I think it's cute. I thought you'd get a kick out of it, I nearly died laughing when I found what had happened.

The baby has pestered me to death about the locket. She yells "Da-Da" and reaches for it every time I'm near her. She has opened (I have for her) so many times I'm wondering if it's made of steel instead of silver. She loves it almost as much as I do. Dianne and Susan want to see Unca Bill in his soldier suit and sweet, you should hear them say their prayers at night. "Please bring Unca Bill and Unca Doc safe home from the war." Dianne is always asking me if you're with the Japs or the Germans. She can't understand, lucky little darling.

Gee, I hope I have a letter from you tomorrow about your experience with the carbine. I'm so thrilled about your "expert's" rating. That's swell, sweet. I wish I could tell you something about me that would make you proud. I'm not even thin anymore. I believe I'm back to 110 or 112. Doggone it, you'll probably never have the opportunity to see me thin and beautiful again!

Nuff nonsense for now, more anon. Will write again tomorrow sweet. Write when and as much as you can. I love you all my life. I've missed you more this week than ever before. Bye now.

Bunch of love,

Mommy

May 16, 1944 – from Missouri Ave, Houston, TX

Monday p.m. (*written on "United Nations Victorious" stationery*)

Dearest,

Just finished listening to Lux Radio Theatre. "Action on the North Atlantic", pretty good, but makes me think too much.

I guess you'll be wondering what on earth is on the back of this sheet. Well, since film and canvas are so scarce I thought I'd try my hand at quick sketches. I know I'm awful but I may be able to improve. I can't explain how she looks in everyday life. There are so many ways about her I wish I could catch for you. Like standing with her hands clasped in the back of her back (what a sentence!) Anyway, I thought you'd get a kick out of your poor wife's efforts. What do you think?

I've really been happy out here at Bobbie's. I've felt so lonely and out of place everywhere else but naturally I miss you more when we start waiting for Theo around five o'clock. But during the day, I'm more like I was at home than anywhere I've been since we broke up our little home. Nuff of this,

I'll tell you what we've done today.

Got up about 7:00 o'clock (so did Bobbie!) and after we breakfasted and cleaned up, we went down to Lily's and washed the clothes. When they finished, we had coffee. They (B and L) went to hang out the clothes and I came home and fed Carol, Susan, Dianne and Jerry. When B and L finished, they came down and boy were they happy to find that over! Anyway, I then fixed cheeseburgers for us and B fixed ice tea. Then, I put Carol to bed and we ate. Susan crawled up on the bed and went to sleep, too! Bobbie then went to the store and when she got back I bathed all 3 squirts and (Carol and Susan, together) then B put on the dinner. I bathed and then she did. Theo came home and rode the kids on the horse. I only wish I could have a camera for that. Oh golly, she's precious on that horse. Not scared a bit on it! Theo rides with her and so far has just walked her. He rides D and S fast and they just die laughing. Just before Carol went to bed, she pointed to the horse and looked up at Theo and said "I wanna ride". She pronounces her "r's" too! S's too. But she still calls Susan, "Di". I could go on and on about her but I must go now. Oh yes, received $80.00 from Uncle Sam today so will put the $48 in the savings bank. Bye now until tomorrow. I love you all my life and can hardly wait to tell you how much.

Kiss yourself the next time you look in the mirror.

Love to you,

Mommy

May 17, 1944 – from Missouri Ave, Houston

Tuesday *(Written on "United Nations Victorious" letterhead)*

Hello again sweetheart,

I say again because I wrote you earlier this evening when I was alone and feeling quite blue. I re-read that letter and have decided our men in the hackie (sp?) have enough readjustments without hearing about their wife's. Anyway, I feel better tonight and am so glad I didn't mail it. I'll tell you the why–for of the situation. We lunched with Clarice Vela today at 1713 Welch. All the old memories came flooding back and I was too weak to take it. I hope we can kinda harden our baby so when she has to take any knocks she can do it like her Dad. Anyway, after we came home, (Carol went to sleep in the car and slept until 4:00!), Bobbie and Lily went to the store. I was here with Dianne, Susan, and Jerry and while they were outside, I decided to take advantage of it and write you. That letter will never go anywhere! You can imagine what it sounds like!

Dorothy called this evening and said Van was scheduled to come home this Saturday but has been transferred to another post and so his leave was cancelled. He was supposed to go out for sea duty so maybe the cancellation and transfer will be alright. Let's hope so. He said in his letter that after three weeks boot training, they'll send you anywhere. Gosh, honey, am glad they didn't accept you in the Navy! They say everything happens for the best so who are we to say anything to the contrary? At any rate, I think you've already fared better than if you'd been in the Navy.

I'm so sleepy I can hardly keep my eyes open. Bobbie and Theo were invited out to a poker party. Lily and Bruce were going and so was Johnny so I offered to keep Jerry. He's a sweet kid and smart as they come. So here I am with Dianne, Susan and Jerry, and our wee bit of heaven – by the way, how did you like the sketches? Do you want me to keep them up? I can't draw her face right so will just leave them alone. You want to see that pudgy little figure anyway! Since I started that, all the kids have bugged me to do theirs. I did Jerry's tonight but Di and Su have been pestering the life out of me (and I love it!) Really, I have enjoyed myself so much. In fact, so much so I don't even want to go home. Awful, aren't I? But it's so cool out here and the baby plays so well with the children. I have more time to really enjoy myself. Of course, home is in Virginia right now and if you'd ask me to come, you can imagine what my answer would be!

Honey, you've never answered my question about taking the baby to an allergist. I don't think she's getting the proper bone and body building materials. If I knew definitely what was causing it, I could do something about it. I can take her to one here, that is, if you prefer him to Balycat.

I'm happy cause I received my $80.00 but a letter from you would make me uncontrollable! I can't kick though, not after the lovely locket and portrait I received Friday and Saturday. I'm going to close now, sweet, this little woman has had a busy day. It feels so good to be fixing dinner and doing dishes again, even if I just help plan and dry for Bobbie. It takes the edge off of the awful homesickness. Write when you can and as much as you can. I love you all my life and missing you terribly –

Love and kisses to you, Poppy,

Your two girls

May 19, 1944 – from Missouri Av, Houston, to Camp Lee, VA

For Wednesday night (written 7 a.m. Thursday morning) – (*written on "United Nations Victorious" stationery*)

My dearest one,

Bobbie and I went to the show last p.m. and had to make the last show so got in pretty late. I was too tired to write anything amusing or entertaining so thought I'd wait until this morning so I could write something you'd enjoy. When Carol was eating breakfast, thought I'd try to catch her for you.

Thursday night: I had to quit, honey, because Dianne woke up and by the time I finished giving her her breakfast Susan woke up. Bobbie got up and while she was feeding her I dressed Carol and helped Dianne dress. Then we started cleaning up and by the time we finished it was time to fix C's lunch. She ate and I put her to bed. Then we put on the ham, fixed potato salad, tomatoes, chives, and fixed the roles to pop in the oven tonite. When we finished bathing and dressing the kids it was time to dress ourselves. Then Bruce, Lily, Johnny, and Jerry came down and we ate. The chicken was playing out on the shell in the driveway and having a wonderful time. The sweet thing, I believe she missed, really missed you, today. I could tell by the way she acted. I couldn't enjoy myself to the utmost either because I kept thinking how much more fun it would have been had you been here to share it. We played gin rummy afterwards. They just left and it's 11:00, so will not make this long.

However, I did not want to tell you about George Harvey. He's leaving Sunday night and I told him to be sure to look up Jim Blatt. I called Janie but she was out so called Sarah. She told me that they hadn't corresponded since you left, so I couldn't get his address. I wondered if you'd ever written him. If so, how is he, and where? Anyway, I'll let you know about George.

I received a letter from my favorite soldier yesterday. It really made me feel good, but I've come to this conclusion. I'm going to be wherever you are, when you are sent to another post or receive your orders. Or at least I hope it's possible I can't make myself be a good readjuster. I try awfully hard, but after having 4 years of heaven, I guess anything would be kinda hard at first. What say? I know you agree.

I'll close now with my poor efforts on the back of the first page and I'll write more tomorrow night, so bye now. I love you all my life.

Yours forever,

Mommy

P.S.: Will send Air Mail stamps when I can get to the P.O.

Baby Ann's May 20th letter

May 20, 1944 – from Houston, TX

Friday p.m.

Hello sweetheart,

Thought I'd make this interesting in so far as I haven't much of interest to say. I do have one thing of importance.

Van is due in here tomorrow about 10:40p.m. Don't you think that's swell? I saw Dorothy today at the bank as I was putting in my $80.00. I hope it won't be too long before I'll have these stars in my eyes! You know I really believe writing this way saves paper. If I'd been writing straight I'd have already used up this page! Oh gosh, just think, I never thought I'd have to do something like this for excitement! I'm just going to write a note tomorrow night because Bobbie and Theo are giving a party and I know I'll be kinda tired at the time. I imagine we'll get to bed. I'll write a long letter Sunday and tell you all about it. I promise to write a real long letter then. I bet you could shoot me for this silly item!

Here's another paragraph – having fun finding out what I have to say? I do want to tell you though that I was invited to dine with Betsy and Bob York and Peggy and Leonard tonite. I made up an excuse because it would make me too lonesome and I'm already pretty much under water anyway. I know one thing, as soon as we can, I'm coming to you. We can work it, I know! Hang the expense. I want my poppy!

Daddy being home has helped a great deal, but makes me want a man of my own! We went over to the Kirklands' this evening. Daddy really likes him. Mrs. K. has been ill again. Kirk seems to be doing fine. I played bridge with Betsy this afternoon. I really enjoyed it. I've also enjoyed staying with Bobbie but, honey. I can't have a good time anymore.

I love you all my life and both your girls miss you terribly. C walks around with your picture - shows it to everybody. I carry your heart in mine and sometimes it hurts – does yours?

I'm going to close this crossword puzzle now. Hope I hear from my favorite soldier boy tomorrow. The time goes so fast at times, but this week it has seemed as though every moment were an hour. 'Scuse this awful letter – will do better Sunday. Bye now. I love you all my life, and I don't know what I'd do if I knew we had to be apart for years. I love you.

Yours,

Mommy

May 22, 1944 – from Houston, TX

Inside the envelope, Ann writes: How I'd love to crawl in bed with you tonite to feel your big arms around me, holding me close. I love you.

Sunday p.m.

Hello sweetheart,

I promised to make up for not writing last night, so will write small so I can get more on less paper so I can send it Air Mail. I just finished writing Doris. I'm sorry I waited so long, but I've been rather lax with my writing since I've been writing you every night. I haven't wanted to write anyone but you. I don't even get excited over my mail anymore from others! <u>Awful, aren't I</u>?

Honey, I had a very good time last night. I would have had a <u>marvelous</u> time if a certain solder had been there. I received your letter and the book and large photograph yesterday and that's another reason I felt good yesterday. Your little note (Wish I could be with you tonight) really thrilled me, sweet, cause I was so lonesome for you before I heard from you that I probably would have gotten drunk and cried all over everybody! I didn't drink much but what I did made me happy. So I enjoyed myself. Everybody saw your picture and the girls all said you were so "nice-looking" or "handsome", or "cute" – they like your looks! I'd better be careful around them when you come back.

Speaking of coming back, John, Mart's husband, is being sent back home. I'll let you know when he arrives in N.Y. and if he's sent to Washington or thereabouts – maybe you could go to see him. I imagine he'll be hospitalized for a few weeks before being discharged, if that's what's going to happen. By the way – that address is 2003 Leak St. Hou.

I'm going to Newgulf Wednesday evening. Pop is coming after us. He didn't want me to drive down by myself. I talked with him this noon and everyone's fine. Today's the 21st so how about writing me there and I'll let you know when to start writing again to 1203, cause if Mama has to keep sending my mail to me, I'll lose a couple a days on lack of letters! I couldn't stand that.

I can hardly wait until we're together again. I didn't know how much you meant to me until now. I'm going to make an effort to be with you after your basic. Remember that. Please tell me what you think. If you don't think it's so hot, let me know and I won't build up my hopes too much. But I'll tell you frankly, sweetheart, that's the only thing that keeps me going. It's plenty tough on you I know, but we're in the same boat now!

The chick is talking so plain now. Yesterday, she asked me for a "coo-kie". I hope those pictures hurry so you can see how precious she really is. She feeds herself now all the time and does it nicely too! When she saw your picture (the big one) today, she held it in her arms and looked out the window – just thinking about you. We both miss you so much.

I'm quitting now, so until tomorrow night, I'll say, good nite, sleep tight, don't let the bed bugs bite (not unless they bite me first) – I love you all my life.

Loads of all I've got –

Yours,

Mommy

Forwarded to New Address: Pvt. William A. Genzer, A.S.N. 38671305, 3512 Ninth Street N.E., Washington, D.C.

May 23, 1944 – from Houston, TX

Inside the envelope, Ann writes: Cuddle up a little closer, lover mine!

Monday p.m.

My dearest one,

I've just had a very pleasant experience. I've been with Dorothy and Van! He looks like he was born in a sailor suit. Really looks good. He had lots of tales to tell so Dorothy calls him a paragraph trooper. He hasn't had a bit of military training although he's finished his boot training and is being transferred upon his return to "Dago" as he calls it. He said he still has your address but just hasn't had time to write. I told him the same was true of your situation so he said he'd probably have more time when he got his transfer so would write then. It made me more lonesome than ever for you.

Pop and Mom are coming after me Wednesday and I thought I'd get Sis' graduation gift for her but I think I'll wait and see what she wants. I want to get her something real nice and thought a small piece of luggage would be nice. If Pop and Mom give her luggage as she wanted, I'll try to match it in a fitted overnight case. Don't you think so? It'll be around $15.00 but she'll only graduate once. What do you think? Answer this right away so I can get it. Don't forget to answer all mail to Newgulf. By the way, they have a phone in now. Call Boling and ask for the residence of Wm Genzer, if you ever want to call.

My country cousin came to see me today. I was quite late and not a little worried since my last period was just a "spotting" one that lasted about three days. But we're sailing clear now so worries are being pushed behind thee, my love.

The baby walked down the whole flight of stairs today by herself! She eats alone and drinks alone. Loves water and drinks all day long. I got a beautiful frame for my lover's picture today and both of us are so proud of it (the picture, not the frame!) I'll go now so be good and careful and write real soon.

I love you all my life.

Yours forever,

Your two girls

May 24, 1944 – from Houston, TX

Tuesday, May 22, 1944

Dearest,

Another day closer to the time when we'll be together again. Gosh, it seems as though that day will never come. I should be ashamed of myself, shouldn't I? We're really very lucky. Anyway, I'd love to find out if you think we'll be able to be near each other after basic. Honey, you said you'd probably know Saturday what branch you'd go into. Since the Army doesn't service its own machines I guess the S.A. deal is out. Kinda nice while it lasted though, eh?

I just finished putting our squirt to bed. It's just about two or four hours since I started this. She was so sweet in her bath, I just decided we ought to be together as long as you're here on this side. Please sweetheart!

I'd love to hear what you're training for. You started Monday, yesterday (May 21st) your technical training, didn't you? Or have I skipped a week somewhere. You're in your seventh week now, aren't you? Or is this the sixth and last week of your military basic?

Another question you've never answered. How long does it take regular mail to get to you? How about Air Mail?

Then there's the question of your zippo lighter. You know I gave it to Theo until you returned. What is your reaction? He is thrilled to death and wants to know about your feelings about the little radio. He wants to know if you want it – he said he'd fix it for you if you did. Speaking about radios, ours is acting up in the same way again. Where did you have it serviced so I can find out if adjustments need to be made? I'd like to know because after all I think he did some pretty bad fixing if you ask me and $10.00 worth at that!

I've got all our clothes ready to throw in to a bag tomorrow so I can be ready when Pop and Mom come tomorrow night for us. I got Mom a hurricane lamp for Mother's Day. It's really beautiful and I know she'll be thrilled with it. The lights go berserk so often out there and all they have are candles so thought it would be a serviceable and lovely gift.

I want to go to the post office tomorrow to get some stamps so I'll send you some Air Mail Stamps then.

I left my card table out at Mildred Buchanan's house the nite of our party. Buck brought it to the office and I went by and picked it up. Everybody's fine and Leonard was in the back office just working away. It made me homesick. I miss you so much. I love you, too, I really think I do!

Well, I'll close this now. I'm trying to listen to the Mobley Theatre (Mysteries) and I guess that's the why – for all the mistakes. Will write tomorrow afternoon here and then day after tomorrow in Newgulf, or rather Cottondale. So bye now and answer all my questions in your next letter. I love you all my life – bye now.

Yours forever,

Your two girls

May 24, 1944 – from Ann in Newgulf, TX, to Camp Lee, VA – forwarded to 9th St., Wash D.C.

Wednesday

Hello sweetheart,

Well, I'm just about all through with my packing. All I have to do is bathe both of us and dress us and put in a few more things and bring them all downstairs and I'll be ready when they come. Wish I was packing for a honeymoon with you. What would it be? Our first was to Austin, our second to New York, our third to Arkansas? I guess it would be our fourth because the other trips we took were with someone else. Well, now that that's settled, we'll be looking forward to our fourth – what say, eh?

The chicken is in bed but is yelling her head off for me. She's starting to cry now. She did the same thing yesterday and slept only about 45 min. I hope she isn't getting out of the habit of those afternoon naps because she's too young. She's not really crying, just fussing and every other breath calling "Mama, Mama!"

She was looking through a magazine today and came across a picture of a soldier. She called me and pointed to it, saying "Da-Da". The sweet thing. She's trying to tear her bed down now. I can hear her.

Warren Tuley's mother called me this noon. Warren's up at Camp Lee and since he knew you were there, wrote for your co. and platoon numbers so he could look you up. In the course of the conversation, we found out she was a very good friend, in fact, chum, of Aunt Mabel's when they were in school. She knew the whole Quattlebaum family and was tickled to know all about each one. Small world, eh?

The chick's quiet now, either she decided to give up and go to sleep or either she found something to do. Hope the bed's far enough away from the wall as she could fast develop a new habit of wall-paper pulling. Here's hoping not!

I'm going to quit now so I can finish up a few things on hand so will say bye now until tomorrow. Be as sweet as you can but save it until I'm with you! So long –

I love you forever,

Mommy

P.S.: Received new address. Both letters arrived today. Hope you're sent within gas limit of Houston – I don't dare hope for too much. I got your Air Mail in one day's time. Hope this reaches you by Friday.

Am now in Newgulf – Everybody fine – missing you – will write a long letter today. I enjoyed your Air Mail so much – I laughed out loud at the sand episode. You never have said anything about the lighter – how about it? Will end now and get this off with the mail man. Am enclosing some Air Mail stamps – hate new address. When you're changed, send Air Mail to let us know. I adore you and am keeping my little fingers crossed!

May 26, 1944, from Ann in Newgulf, TX

Aunt Marie is Ann's mother's older sister, Marie Regina Mouton Terry, 61.
Memere refers to Momo's mother, Philomene Cora Louaillier Mouton, who had died two years before.

Inside the envelope, Ann writes: "Dream of me tonight, my love – I'll try to dream of you."

Thursday
May 25, 1944

Hi sweetheart,

Here I am at the old homestead. We arrived last p.m. about 10:30. Had a pleasant drive in but the chick woke up when we got here. I put her on the pot and after she finished I put her to bed. She went right back to sleep. When we started looking, Sis' graduation gifts over (she got some lovely things!), she (Carol) decided she wanted to get up. I brought her in here and she stayed awhile, then I put her to bed once more and this time she stayed. That is until about 1:00. It started pouring down rain and Mom got up to look after the chickens. She turned on the light in the sun porch and that's what woke Carol. She got in bed with Sis and I and slept the rest of the night. I guess that about winds up our little journey to "Cottondale" for the time being.

Four generations, c. 1940: Philomene Cora Louaillier Mouton, known by family as Memere, 83; Sarah Ann Mouton Quattlebaum, 48; Effie Roberta Quattlebaum Frank, 22; and Roberta Dianne Frank, 9 months.

In my last night's letter, I mentioned how much I enjoyed your air mail of yesterday. I read it to the folks and we all got a kick out of the wheelbarrow and sand episode. Yes, my sweet, this technical training is really something! I think the episode of your beginning to smoke again is something to remember. That's cute! Do you want your lighter – I told Theo and Bobbie said "Honey, you'd better send Bill his lighter. He'll probably want it now." Whereupon, Theo turned to me with "Tell that bastard he's S.O.L.". I bit and asked what S.O.L. meant – "S (like in the 5 S's) out of luck! " I nearly died!

I told you I read your letter to the folks but I omitted the part which interested me most about the dream. Oh, golly, I tried to dream about you but I just couldn't last night. I guess I was just a wee bit too tired. You know how I sleep when once I get started!

Mrs. Tuley, Warren's mother, called me yesterday. Warren's in Camp Lee and wrote her for your address. I have his in case you want to look him up before you're shipped. It's Prvt. Warren D. Tuley, A.S.N. 38671825, Co. "N", 13th A.S.F.T.R. Camp Lee, Virginia. I didn't mean to put that in (*she includes an arrow pointing to Camp Lee*), I imagine you know that part! I was copying it and just kept right on. Mrs. Tuley said she'd made him some cookies and date sticks and said to be sure and tell you to hurry over to see him so you can get some, too. The sugar situation is a little better here so you will be getting a package next week, too. After we had talked awhile, Mrs. Tuley asked me if I was any kin to Mabel and Robert Quattlebaum. (She got the name from Frankie when she called to find out how to get in touch with me.) Come to find out she was a chum of Aunt Mabel's when they were at Hawthorne! I know I'm repeating but I had so little time yesterday I just had to outline a few things.

Well, the big news down our way is Carita left Benton. Carita says it's just a visit to Marie's but a little birdie told me better. I wish she'd make up her mind. She's too used to luxury to change at this late date. Aunt Marie can't give her the things she's used too, not since Memere's death, anyway.

Benton is supposed to come in Friday for the wrestling matches with Uncle Ben. I should know a few more details by then. Oh, I forgot, I'm not in Houston, that will have to wait until I return, but I'll gather up all the dirt and send it to you.

Your mother just brought in a white vase filled with red roses. She put them right by your picture and looked up and said to me "I'm giving our Pvt. William some red roses – tell him that!" We're very proud of our soldier and all of us are holding our breath for further news from you.

So until then, I'll quit. I'm just kidding cause you know (and so do I), I'll be writing again tomorrow.

It's about 20 after eleven and many hours and many things have happened since I started to stop this. I'll tell you all about it tomorrow. We just got back from the Chapman's. We played "42" and I really enjoyed it. We took the baby and put her on the bed in the next room with the door <u>open</u> and she slept through it all! Just like she used to do! I'll quit now and write all about it tomorrow. I love you all my life.

Bye now –

Always yours,

Mommy

May 26, 1944

Aunt Martha is Matilda "Tillie" Genzer's younger sister, 43 years old. Winifred is Aunt Martha's daughter-in-law, who married Martha's second son Lawrence Edward Ripper in 1943.
Mom and Pop refer to Bill's parents, Willie and Tillie, 47 and 45 respectively, and Sis refers to Bill's little sister, Lorraine, 17 years old.
Opa and Oma are Tillie's parents, George Friedrich Brandt, 62, and Julia Hickel Brandt, 59, (Bill's maternal grandparents.)

May 26, 1944
Friday
Graduation Nite

Hi sweet,

I'm just going to have to start this tonite anyway, but I promise I'll finish it tomorrow. It's about 1:30 now and our little sister is a graduate. Aunt Martha and Opa and Oma came in about noon today for the celebration. She has received so many lovely things. I've got so many things to tell you I'll probably have to wait and write some of the things some day when nothing's happened. I'm going to say goodnite now cause I'm really sleepy. Be sweet. I love you all my life and miss you just lots. I'll tell you all about that when I see you and make your dreams come true. Bye for now – I love you.

Saturday morn:
Aunt Martha took the baby this morning when she woke up and I slept until after ten. Second time since you left! It really felt good. They even gave her her breakfast. Wasn't that swell!

Well, I'll begin with Thursday night. The Chapman's asked us over for 42 and we went. I put the baby to bed about 8 and when we got ready to leave, I just picked her up and we went on over. She woke up when we got there and stayed awake just long enough to look around. I put her on the big bed in the room adjoining the living room and with the doors open and all the noise, she kept right on sleeping. Here's a diagram: (*Ann draws a "floor plan" picture of a bed with Carol on it, then an open door and then two card tables in the next room.*) We were playing at the card table and the radio was blaring and we were shouting and laughing and boy, was I proud of our little girl! When we got ready to leave, we picked her up, put her in the car, drove home, and put her in her bed and she slept <u>all</u> <u>night</u>!

Well, then Friday morning, Opa and Oma arrived with Aunt Martha and we went to the graduation exercises. It was beautiful. I didn't take the baby because Emma was here and she stayed with the baby. She's just the type you'd like. Kinda like Louise, but weighs close to 200 pounds. A black mama if I ever saw one. Carol really liked her. I put her to bed and then left. Emma said she coughed once and the rest of the time was quiet as a little mouse! She said, "Dat baby is <u>too</u> good!" I really laughed.

Opa and Oma left pretty early this morning but Aunt Martha is still here. We're taking her home tomorrow.

Carol just walked over to the table with the four red roses and your picture on it. She picked up the picture, kissed it and walked away! Try to picture it – it's just precious!

I hope I can get some news of what's going on with the better and more complete of myself. I may get something today, who knows?

Aunt Martha said a very lovely compliment to your weaker half. Mother's Day they were talking about daughter-in-laws. You know Winifred is expecting a baby in October – I think I told you that. Well anyway, Aunt Martha said she only had one real daughter-in-law and that was me. Don't you think that's a pretty swell tribute to your wife? I do! Mom told me this yesterday and she also said that someone told Aunt Martha that maybe someday she'd get a daughter-in-law like me and when Aunt Martha said no, it couldn't be possible, Sis said, "They threw away the mold after they made her." Honey, you just don't know what this means to me. Or I guess you do, at that anyway. I thought you'd be as happy and proud when you heard it as I was. They all miss you and are all so proud of "Sonny".

I'm going to close now so I can feed the chick. This is Friday's letter so thought I'd get it off on that 1:00 mail truck. I'll write more tonight but what I don't know. No telling with this outfit – anything can happen! But look who <u>I'm telling</u>!

I love you and am awaiting anxiously for a bit of news. Bye now. I love you just oodles –

Always yours,

Your two girls

May 27, 1944

Saturday

<u>For You</u>

I do believe that God above
Created you for me to love;
He picked you out from all the rest,
Because he knew I'd love you best.
I once had a heart called "mine", 'tis true,
But now it's gone from me to you;
Take good care of it, as I have done,
For you have two and I have none.
If I go to heaven and you're not there,
I'll paint your face on the Golden Stair;
So all the angels can know and see,
Just what you really mean to me.
If you're not come by judgment day,
I'll know you've gone the other way;
So I'll give the angels back their wings,
Their golden harp and everything;
And just to show you what I'd do –
I'll go to Hell, dear, just for you.

Your Own,

Mommy

May 28, 1944

George is Aunt Martha's oldest son, George Frank Ripper. Not sure of others mentioned and their relationship.

Inside the envelope, Ann writes: I'll be loving you always – not for just an hour, not for just a day, not for just a year, but always.

Dearest one,

Of course, you can imagine my excitement over the telegram. It caused no little stir around the loved ones either, for that matter. Pop opened it when he received it and they brought it home when he came last night. I wanted to write right away, but I went to the show in Wharton. I dashed off a copy of a poem I thought you'd enjoy because it sounded like it was meant for us. Anyway, to get back to the telegram, I didn't have an address so will wait and send these letters when you send it. I'm dying of curiosity to know what you're doing. I'm really glad you're getting to see the "big city", as everyone calls it here. Naturally, I can't help but be a little excited knowing the possibilities of the move. It may seem a long ways from each other but still there isn't an ocean between us and as long as this condition holds I can take anything. Can't help but hope, though, we may be together before too long. I guess you're as much that way as I, though.

Everything is fine down this way. We took Aunt Martha home this a.m., and just got back. It's about 10:00 and we dressed the chick for bed in the car so when we came in, I didn't disturb her, just dumped her in bed. She made quite a bit with everybody. Erna and Nina were there and, of course, Uncle Willie. George was there also and we spent the greater part of the day playing bridge. I really enjoyed it. He can play auction but not contract and although Aunt Martha, Sis, and I play contract, we had to play auction. Still I enjoyed it very much. When we were on our way there, we stopped to see Uncle Powell and Aunt Mary. She doesn't look well since she hasn't been very well lately but Powell hasn't changed a bit since I first met him. They're both fine now. Carol was really a showboat over at their house and I was so proud of her. She's a cute little devil and really takes advantage of it. Her hair has been a sensation to all your kin–folks and they just can't help exclaiming over it.

I'm in a pretty bad position – hope you can read this. I'm half lying down and sitting up on the couch in the sun porch. Mom and Pop are out doing their daily dozens with the chickens. We brought back a calf with us from Aunt Martha's in the trunk of the car. It wasn't bad, either! Sis has a date, rather Bruce saw us drive in and came over so they went somewhere. The chick and I are alone here in the house and I know she's dreaming of her Daddy and when we're all together again. I dreamed last night, we were just like your dream last Sunday night and right after I woke up I remembered it and said to myself I wouldn't forget so I could tell you tonight but that's the way I am with dreams, you know. Swell while they last but they don't last long enough.

I'm going in to undress now and wash my face and teeth so I'll be out of the bathroom when Pop and Mom come in. I think of you constantly and pray for so much. I love you, sweetheart, and want you – terribly.

Yours forever and ever,

Mommy

P.S.: Wish I'd look up now and see you standing by the door yelling for me to put on the frying pan. You're coming in with a couple of fryers. We didn't know what we had, did we?

May 28, 1944 (date of letter) – from Pvt. A.E. Genzer, A.S.N. 38554290, Co. A 78th Engineer Bn., A. P.O. 847, c/o Postmaster, Miami, FL
Via U.S. Army Postal Service, postmarked May 30, 1944

Fred is Bill's 1st cousin, Alfred Emil "Slim" Genzer, son of Joseph Genzer, Jr. Fred is 19 years old at the time he writes this letter.

May 28, 1944
Puerto Rico

Dear Bill,

Just a few lines to let you know that I received your letter a few days ago. I am sorry I didn't get to answer any sooner. But we were out in the field and didn't get back until yesterday. Today is another lonesome Sunday. I spend most of the day sleeping. I am not feeling so good. I caught a cold again. And have a headache with it. I was going to take some pictures this afternoon, but it rained and the sun didn't want to come out. I don't believe I'll be able to take any today.

How are you getting along, hope fine?

So you like the army pretty good so far. But miss your wife and baby. Well, you will forget about that before long. I know how it was when I came in. Boy, I wish I could be thinking about going home soon. I wasn't at home for so long, I would be lost if I would get back. And won't get back for a long time. Not sooner than two years. Well, Bill, I hate to do this, but I'll have to close for today. I have so many letters to answer I don't know which one to start first. So goodbye and good luck until next time.

Your cousin,

Fred

May 29, 1944 – from Ann, Newgulf, TX

Monday night

Dearest,

How's my soldier this evening? Wish I knew more about him – then maybe I could write a more interesting letter. This is the fifth you'll get at once. The first was Friday's because I started it Friday night and by the time I'd finished it, your telegram came and I decided to wait and send them all at the same time. When I get your address, I'll mail these regular mail but will Air Mail the one I write after I hear from you. I've dated them all on the envelope so you can read them in the succession they were written.

Sis, who, by the way, has even Pop calling her Lorraine now – has gone to a dance at Palacious (sp?) – Camp Helen, anyway. She left just before five and will come back about midnight. I think they're supposed to leave Camp at 12:00. She wanted me to go with them but, heck, even if it didn't look funny, I wouldn't enjoy myself. Every time I see a boy in uniform, I could just eat worms, so you have nothing to worry about on this end. Of course, the U.S.O. and all that are up your way but that's different and I know what I mean to you, so don't be afraid to do anything you want. See, babe – I trust you!

I had so much I wanted to tell you and now can't think of a thing. I just put our baby to bed so I'll stop now and fix supper so when Pop and Mom come in, we can go ahead and eat – Tootlehonkle for now, lover.

'Tis now 11pm and all's well with us. I fixed chili and the last jar, by the way. It was delicious and I couldn't help thinking of Lake Poncitrain and how green you looked! Oh, golly, wasn't that something! Hope we have many more silly memories – even if they are distasteful at the time.

Mom just asked me if I mailed those other letters. After I said no, she said, "Are you going to put them all in one envelope?" I quickly replied that you'd probably get more kick out of a lot of mail rather than just one big one.

I weighed today and I've lost another pound. 106 now! Your wife is getting thin and beautiful, but darn it, I can't keep this up long – you'd better hurry up and send for me so you can see how your wife looks. I'll get fat again if you don't! Seriously though, I do hope this means something – about your Washington post, I mean. I think you're there in a bureau taking your technical, but of course, there's always the chance you may be stationed there long enough for a visit from me or a furlough for you before too long. I'm not raising my hopes and although I may speak of coming up there, I want you to know I understand the situation and wouldn't do anything foolish. I'm waiting on you and if the chance for our being together occurs, I know darn well how you'd jump at it. So until that time, I'm willing to wait – and pretty patiently too for a beautiful, thin person.

I'm about to fall out writing this so think I'll quit and hit the hay. My eyes feel as though they were made of lead and I imagine you know the feeling only too well these days, eh?

Mom and Pop are already in bed and sitting here alone kinda has its drawbacks, so if you don't mind I believe I'll end this poor specimen of a letter and lay the body down.

Hope I get a letter tomorrow – hope, hope, hope!

I love you all my life.

Yours forever –

Mommy

P.S.: Your precious baby picked up your picture today and I asked her who it was – she said "Boy", and I said "Is that your boy friend?" She replied, "Uh huh – Mama's boy!" Pretty smart gal for only a year and seven months!

I love you, M.

May 30, 1944 – from Newgulf, TX

Hello sweetheart,

It's close to 10:00pm and we just finished dinner. We've really had a day today. We didn't have gasoline for the pump yesterday so had to put off washing until this morning. Emma came this afternoon and as fast as Mom could get the clothes out on the line and get them partly dry, Emma would iron. In the meantime, besides taking care of the chicken, Sis, pardon me – Lorry – and I cleaned house and cleaned the floors with Bruce cleaner, then put on Bruce wax and polished with an electric polisher – so you can see now this isn't going to be a very long letter.

I did want to tell you though I received the picture and Air Mail you sent after the telegram. Evidently you haven't received my change of address. I thought you had but I guess the telegram was forwarded by Aunt Tennie. It had retained the Camp Lee heading so I naturally thought you knew I was here. But when I got the picture and letter with Mother's handwriting forwarding it, I knew, of course.

Speaking of the picture – Honey, I love you and think you're awfully pretty but I think you look awful in it. However, you're still the best looking in the whole outfit and I'm not the only one who thinks so. A bunch of Lorry's girl friends were over this evening and that's what they said!

Another thing, my friend! A WAC camp, eh! Tell me more – this has really got me worried and another thing, if you can't find me a decent fountain pen (with a blunt point), I don't know how long these letters will be. If I have to fight with it much more I'll have a bum right arm when you come home!

I'm tired, sweet, so I'm going to close. I love you but next time you take a picture – smile!

I miss you tonight very much.

All my love (except the amount I have for our little girl),

Mommy

May 31, 1944 – from Ann in Newgulf, TX, to 9th St. in DC

This letter includes the commencement program from Boling High School with Lorraine Genzer's name as one of the graduates. The commencement took place on May 26, 1944 at 9:00pm at the Boling Athletic Field.

Wednesday

Hi Sweet,

It's 4 p.m. and all's well, the wind's from the South and it's hot as hell!

Nice beginning, eh wot? I'm starting this now because I have a few minutes before I get ready to go get Pop. We kept the car today but didn't get to do anything because we found out we couldn't see Aunt Frances until tomorrow or the next day. She was operated on yesterday morning if I failed to mention it. However, she's doing as well as can be expected. I don't know yet what all was done but will report just as soon as I do. Henrietta came in yesterday but haven't seen her yet.

I'm going to get ready now and we're going to get Pop so bye now until tonite – Hope there's an Air Mail for me at the Post Office. That's where we're going first. Until tonight, then – I love you!

Wednesday

Dearest,

I was so thrilled to hear from you. The telegram arrived this morning, but I didn't get it until late this p.m. Pop got it this a.m. but forgot we had a telephone! Anyway, I'm just dying of curiosity to know what your "job" is and what the set up means. I'm Air Mailing this to let you know I know what's going on. This is the second letter I've started today, so I'll just put the first sheet of the early letter with this. I also received a letter from Aunt Tennie. Theo has been deferred until November. I imagine the Franks are all quite excited – don't you – and the Genzers are quite that way too, if you get what I mean!

I started writing this with my pen and I'm now writing you with Lorry's. How you like that hint!

I'm going to bring this to a close with a little incident that happened today. The baby picked her phone up and said "Hi, Dada – uh huh –buy" and I asked her if she called you and she picked up the phone again and said – "gone " – so I guess she meant she'd talked to you but you had already hung up! Sweet little thing!

Bye again, and I love you all my life –

Yours forever,

Mommy

P.S.: I'm sending by regular mail the letters I've written since I had no address for you – By again. - Love you, M

June 2, 1944 – from Newgulf, TX

Thursday

Hello popsy,

Another day gone. No letter but I'm pretty sure there will be one tomorrow. I still haven't received the letter you wrote after you wired the second time. When Pop came home this evening without it, I said that if it was there at noon tomorrow to call me. Then I said that would make it worse 'cause we wouldn't have the car so I told him not to. He then said he'd come home at noon and bring it if it were there. I said that was foolish, then he informed me he wanted to know what was in it as much as I did. He just told me to be sure and tell you he was sure working hard. He's so tired – he plowed this afternoon until "that darn little plow played out" – he was so mad! We nearly died laughing. You know how excited he gets when anything goes wrong!

Say sweet – I really like my pen now. You know how scratchy it was? Well, look at it now! Sis cleaned it up for me last p.m. after I wrote you with her pen. So don't get the fountain pen. I don't need it now. However, you've never mentioned the radio. If you want it, send for it and Theo will get it fixed up for you and send it. If you happen upon any batteries, you could use mine. It's not bad either. It's a good little radio, and I'd really like it if you used it. Of course, the batteries is another thing. But do let me know.

Yesterday, Sis and I went after Pop yesterday and after we got the mail, Sis started reading a letter from the Texas Co. to Pop. (This was after we'd stopped and had beer and cakes.) Guess who had the beer! Anyway, the letter started off with "It's spring" – and Sis read it like it should and just about then I started whistling "Spring Song" and we got tickled. Well, we laughed and laughed. Pop couldn' t see anything funny and after we stopped giggling, he said from now on he was going to start drinking cokes! Well, you can imagine what that started. We laughed all the way home!

I was about out of ink so had to stop to get the tank filled. That's all you can get filled today!

The chicken is a mess and every time Mom or Pop go out to the back, she has a fit to go out with them. She's really getting big. Says what she wants and gets what she wants too. She isn't spoiled though. I' ve had a hard job on both sides, but I believe I've done it. Aunt Martha thought I was cruel when I wouldn't do something the baby wanted, or when I put her to bed and she'd cry or something like that. But she was here only three days and we took her home on the fourth and the little darling was perfect. They couldn't get over her and also her hair as I've said before.

Mom just said to tell you that I'm writing all the news and she'll write later. She's so tired – she really works too hard, honey – but I guess everyone is these days.

Pop just said if you need anything let him know. He also wants to know what kind of cigarettes you smoke. Don't fail to answer this, sweet, because they want to do something for you. They really have been swell to me and I'll never forget it. It's just little things, but you know how much little things mean to me. I did want to ask you if you needed any toilet articles, razor blades, soap, socks, handkerchiefs - you name it, you'll have it. I saw some shaving lotion – aftershave, I mean and I thought if you needed it I could go ahead and get it. It's pretty hard to find Williams stuff in Houston, so let me know.

How do you like my stationery? If you'd like to have some, or any stationery, that is, I'll send you that too. The fridge will have to wait again, sweet, because the peaches are coming in and so are the plums but just as soon as we're through with them – (another three or four days), we'll send some divinity too!

I'm going to quit now. It's between 10:00 and 10:15 and "I Love a Mystery" is on. I haven't heard it in ages, and it makes me a wee bit homesick. That theme song stirs so many memories. 1713, and jumping up and dashing to the bathroom so we could get to bed early - oh, shut up.

I'll probably Air Mail one tomorrow night and so I'll just send this by regular mail. Bye now.

I love you all my life -

Your Mommy

June 3, 1944 – to 9th St in DC, from Newgulf

Friday

Dearest,

I thought I'd start this because it seems every time I start one in the afternoon, I get a letter from you that evening – so here goes.

The peaches are in the pot ready to boil away and Sis just finished making some ice cream. If this keeps up we may even make some candy for a certain soldier who's holding down a "job" with the War Dept in D.C. – Do you happen to know him? He's usually called "honey" or "sweetheart", or "sonny" – and is a cute little devil! At least his wife thinks so. (Not so little though – is he?) Speaking of names – Pop usually calls me "Darling" now and yesterday he said his next wife was going to be like me – of course we were speaking of the price of permanents in USA – but I don't think that had anything to do with it – do you?!!!

I wish 6 p.m. would hurry and come. Pop will be home and I may have read a letter that will tell me a few things about my husband.

By the way, I took a nap after noon and dreamed of you. It was a very ordinary dream but I was with you for a tiny little while, anyway!

I'll quit now and finish this tonite. I love you all my life.

Oh, sweetheart, if you could have seen me when I read your letter. Pop came home about 5:30 and yelled at me that I had a letter from Bill. I read it out loud (not all of it but just the parts that would interest them). Anyway, when I came to the part where you said it may be possible we could live together – I could hardly speak – I can't remember when I've been happier. I'll tell you all about it in a month. Maybe we'll be together to celebrate my birthday. My fingers are crossed and you can imagine how I'm praying! By the way, be sure and look up May Quattlebaum – she's in the Post Office Dept but I don't know any more than that. Try the Telephone Directory. She may be able to help find us a place. One room, a hot plate and bathroom are all we need for Heaven.

I've spent most of the day looking at a map of D.C. and trying to find out whether this address is where you work or live. Where do you work? What building? I've read the letter out loud three times and have one more to go (to Mom) and then I'll start reading it to myself. Golly, I've wanted this for so long and now that it's here it doesn't seem long at all!

Here I am talking of our being together and not even mentioning the good luck that made it possible. I guess you know your little family is very proud of you – not saying anything about you, big one. I'm still shaking so if this sound a bit screwy (oh golly, even the word makes me jump!), don't mind me!

I'm going to quit now and write to Mama. I told the chicken we were going to Washington and live with Daddy and I asked her if it was alright with her. Her little eyes got so big and she said "Uh, huh!" and clapped her little hands together. She's gotten so big, sweet, you'll really be surprised. I'm just hoping it won't be too long before we can have that happy meeting. I have so many things to tell you, we'll be trying to find time to sleep – oh, I forgot – I'll have a night owl for a husband!

Bye for now – until tomorrow night and I forgive you for not writing since you wired and then wrote such lovely news. Tell me more about your roommate – do you like him? Is he married and is his wife coming up? Tell all –

I love you all my life and am very happy tonight,

Your Mommy

P.S.: Aren't you a pvt any longer? You'd better start putting your rating on the return address!!

June 4, 1944 – from Ann in Newgulf, TX, to 9th St. in DC

Saturday p.m.

Hiya George,

Your wife is a very happy person at the present time. I've done nothing today except plan. I have so many things to tell you that when I see you, goodness knows what will happen. Golly, honey, it still sounds like I'm dreaming! Pinch me, too, somebody!

Sis and I just got back from Wharton. We had to get some chicken feed. Growing mesh for the ones outside and fruit and Jello for the little one inside! I got some pretty material and so did Sis. She got a pattern and we're both going to use it. Mine is watermelon and hers is purple. It's the same print, only the colors differ. Hope you like it!

We're going to express the alarm clock but Pop is going to make a box for it. We don't want the same thing happening to it that happened to your cake! If you could wait, I might bring it up, with me! Oh boy – doesn't that sound swell! No kidding though, we'll get it off next week – first thing.

I wrote Oma and Opa today and I also wrote Jean a note. I wanted to give Joe your address but I couldn't tell him any more so maybe you'd better drop the office a line.

I had so many things I wanted to tell you but now I seem to have forgotten them all.

I do want to know more about you and the situation there. Let me know as soon as you know and try to find a place for us – (isn't that grand!) Anyway, oh, but I know you'll do all you can – and as soon as you can, too.

Mom just stuck her head in the door and said "Tell Bill to be a good boy until you get there" and Sis said "What do you think he'll do – be a bad boy when Anne gets there?" She don't know you very well – do she?!!! Whew!

I've got to go now. I'm tired – Been ironing all day – think I'll go sit on the back porch and suck an orange – (with an accent, of course!)

I love you all my life and am so thrilled and excited, I can't begin to tell you. However, I hope it won't be long before I can rattle on and on and on!

Say honey – do you get any days off? The aspect of grand children will be very low – you working nites and all – but of course daylight never bothered us before, did it – better burn this before one of your chums gets ahold of it!!

Bye now –

Sleep tight and hold on just a little while longer.

I love you,

Your Mommy

June 5, 1944 – from Ann in Newgulf, TX, to 9th St. in DC

Sunday

Hello Sweetheart,

I just put the chick to bed for the night and thought I'd sit down and start your letter and maybe – for once – I won't start it at midnight.

I've been thinking of so many things. Out of my happiness and great excitement over recent developments, I find sleep very hard to come to me. During these hours of thought, I find myself going over a few things which will have to be attended to when I join you. Naturally since we won't know for sure for a little while I hate to count my chickens but here goes anyway.

First, about the car. I think the best thing would be dead storage. Then if the occasion arises that we need the money, then we could sell. This is just my idea of course, as are all of these items. You know what's best but I've never kept out of your affairs, so why should I try now!

Secondly, there's the apt (oh thrill!) Of course, that's another thing and knowing a little of the housing situation in D.C. I'm rather reluctant to count on anything at first but a room, (if that!)

Anyway, I still have a few sheets and other linens over at Mama's. I was intending to bring them down here this trip but since I spent last week with Bobbie, it made short stuff of time. Anyway, we don't have to bother about winter things. If the war is still on, I hope we're lucky enough to still be there – in which case we can always send for the stuff. Another thing – we don't have a piece of everyday dishes – only our good china. I was thinking it would be better to buy a cheap set from Sears and have it there when I get there (oh glory!!) I can dig out some knives and forks but if not, we can always buy a few. Then – we don't have to worry about kitchen utensils. Except for my frying pan, she has enough to do for us. Kitchenware, too. (Knives, etc.)

Once you think it's ok and can find a place, it won't take this one long to get there. When you find a place – please wire me – then write about it. Honey, I don't care what it looks like just so it's clean enough for our chicken. To keep her well is awfully important, but <u>look</u> who I'm telling <u>that too</u>!

Golly, popsy, I still have my doubts. Do you really think I can come or do you know? I hope you write tonite and I'm enclosing – oh no, I'm not – I have to go to the P.O. tomorrow – only one, no, two Air Mails left and I'd better keep one in case we don't keep the car tomorrow.

Pop and I both ran out of cig (*cigarettes*) this morning. Sis went to see "a guy named Joe" (that sounds funny – doesn't it!) this noon and she's supposed to bring us some back – here it is almost 8pm and still no weeds – wish I had a nice butt (no cracks, please!)

I'll quit now cause here comes Sis. Will write again tomorrow and boy! Am I praying!!

I love you all my life, my love, be sweet and – it's hard to wait – but think when we're together in our own place with our baby again – oh golly – it's swell. I went to church in Newgulf this morning and offered my Mass to a Thanksgiven (*sic*) for everything, especially your life in the Army. I want to go to Communion Sunday (or sooner if possible for it.) How about you going to Communion next Sunday too and we'll make our Thanksgiving together. We have so much and others have so little.

I love you, my darling,

Your own two girls

P.S.: Did you get a deluge of letters – the ones I wrote when I didn't know your address?

Hello again,

Pop and Mom are out doing their evening chores and Sis went to League so thought I'd dash off a few more words. I wanted to know if you get any extra money for board and room – if so that would help a great deal. With your $27.00 and my $80.00, that's $107.00 (we can do it cause don't you get a physician's care free of charge and your family, too?) That's the biggest item in my budget – dr's fees and medicines. She's taking a new vitamin now – it costs 2 bucks per bottle and I have to keep cough medicine, nose drops, epicac, and a car load of drugs on hand all the time. I'm not kicking, tho, cause if they prevent illness that's ok by me – how about you? She eats just about everything we do so baby food would be a small item compared to what it used to be. We can't do much, but just being with you is all I need (with a deck of cards and some poker chips, maybe.)

I'm going to close now. We taught Pop to play gin rummy the other nite and he just came in with a pack of cards so he wants to try a hand. Bye again,

I love you,

Mommy

June 6, 1944 – from Ann, P.O. Box 142, Newgulf, TX

Historical Note: This letter was written on D-Day.

Monday (*Wednesday was written above Monday, then crossed out*)

Dearest,

I received your letter of the 3rd and I was thrilled all over again. When can I be ready when you give me the "come on"? Well, I'll tell you. If we're to live in a place where we won't need linen, utensils and such – I can pack my clothes and the baby's and get on the train by the time a letter could reach you saying I'm on my way. However, if it's the other, it'll take me about four or five days before I get on the train. Another thing is finding a place for me. Could we stay where you are or are you trying (or have you found) another place? Either way, it would be a week or ten days after I receive the signal from you when I'd be kissing you – (oh, chill!)

I'm still dopey – as any fool can plainly see!

Pop just drove by the front door driving a team of horses. He's going to rake the alfalfa. He had it cut yesterday evening. Mr. Helms did it and they (his wife and son) are very nice. I really do like them. She's been over here before though. I've never met him though. He's nice looking, isn't he?

This is a bit off our beaten track though so will go back to previous conversation (oh, yum!)

I'm going to start my watermelon dress (it's loud but you'll love it!) in a few minutes. When I finish it, I'll just have one more dress to make and I want to make a hat, buy a bag, and I'm fixed! The chick has oodles of summer clothes so that's taken care of. I'll have to find a friend in D.C. with a sewing machine if we're there this winter – (oh, tush!)

Speaking of Washington – you (after asking how long it would take me to get ready), you mentioned something about – "that is, if you'd like to live in Washington, D.C." – Ha Ha! Are you kidding? Remember the little poem I sent you? Does that answer that?

Honey, do you realize we'll be seeing the place together that we've always wanted to visit – and it'll only cost us half as much! I realize the circumstances are quite different than we'd anticipated but nevertheless that's the fact. I imagine you know a little about it – do you think you could guide a war wife and war chicken around the "Big City"? Or wouldn't you like that?

Answer all these questions as soon as you get this so I can start arrangements. If you're thinking of finding a place, start <u>now</u>! (If you're in the latrine enjoying one of the 5 S's – I'm only kidding!)

I'm going to quit now so I can finish my sewing so in case I get a letter within the next few days (from a guy named Bill) saying "Come up and see me soon – no – right <u>now</u>!)

I love you all my life –

Yours forever,

Mommy

P.S.: I'm going to have to have the little locket welded on – your daughter yanks it off every time I wear it and yells – "Da Da". I think she knows we're coming to you – she's happier and is sleeping all night in her own little bed. (By the way, I'm expressing the clock so don't think that's your Father's Day gift) – Love, Mommy

---

June 6, 1944 – from Ann, Newgulf, TX
Historical Note: This letter was written on D-Day.

The letter was a greeting card for Father's Day, "To My Husband, With Love on Father's Day"

There isn't any Husband's Day
On which to wish you well
So I'll just pick out Father's Day
To say, "I think you're swell!"

Your two girls

Note: Ann crossed out I and wrote We.

June 6, 1944 – from William and Matilda Genzer, Bill's parents
Historical Note: This letter was written on D-Day.

The letter included a greeting card for Father's Day, "To a Father in the Service on Father's Day"
Inside card, it reads:
Though you're away on Father's Day
Remember this, please do,
That you'll be wished the very best
And thought of all day through!

Mom and Pop

Tue. noon, June 6

Dear Son,

Just a few lines for today. Am glad to hear you got a job with the War Dept. and hope you like it.

We are thinking of you every day. Since Ann writes every day and tell you all the news, I have not much to write and am glad she writes every day so you have all the news.

Pop is making hay again. We are all just fine, hope you are too. You be good and take care of yourself. Will have to stop and get this off.   Will write more later.

Bye and Love,

Mom and Pop

June 7, 1944 – from Ann, Newgulf, TX, to 3512 Ninth St., N.E., Wash DC

On outside of envelope, Bill wrote "D-Day" in the corner probably as a reminder of this historic day, and Ann references the event in her letter below.

Inside the envelope, Ann writes: "You're the swellest husband in the world and I'll be telling you all about it very soon in person!!"

Tuesday
June 6, 1944

My darling popsy,

I wanted to mail this when I mailed a card to you sooner but couldn't find time before the mailman was due. So I'll dash off a note now to tell you that your Father's Day gift is a little delayed so it'll be about Friday before I can mail it. I mean express it. I'll explain later why I have to go now. It's too involved and Pop needs me now.

Well, I'm back. I've been driving the car and trailer around while Pop and a Mexican threw it on. They were putting it in the shed when I started this.

I can go no further. I've got to mention the thing that everyone is so excited about. Mrs. Helms called us about 4 a.m. this morning and told us to turn on the radio. Pop got all excited and dashed in to turn the radio on. When we heard what had happened – well, you can imagine our excitement! No more sleep for anyone but Carol and me (you know me and sleep!) (Almost as close to you and me!)

We were wondering if you had anything to do with the news agency. Since you're on the teletype it sounds plausible then again, I know you don't get the news first in your office – but – oh, I'm getting all mixed up. I mean maybe you were the one who got the flash from the Washington News Agency into your office. There! Now do you see what I mean?

Anyway, the whistles all around here were blowing their heads off when the early shifts went on (between 5:00 and 6:30).

I'm going to close now cause I want to work on my watermelon pink dress so I can wear it the first time you see me (or would you rather see me in my suit). You've never seen either one. I look snazzy in my suit!

Be sweet and I'll see that your Father's Day gift gets there soon. I love you all my life and oh golly, when I see you!!!!!

Bye now,

Your own,

Mommy

(Then a note was added at the bottom from Carol, in her handwriting, but clearly with Ann helping her.)

You're the sweetest Daddy in the world and I want to see you. Love, Carol

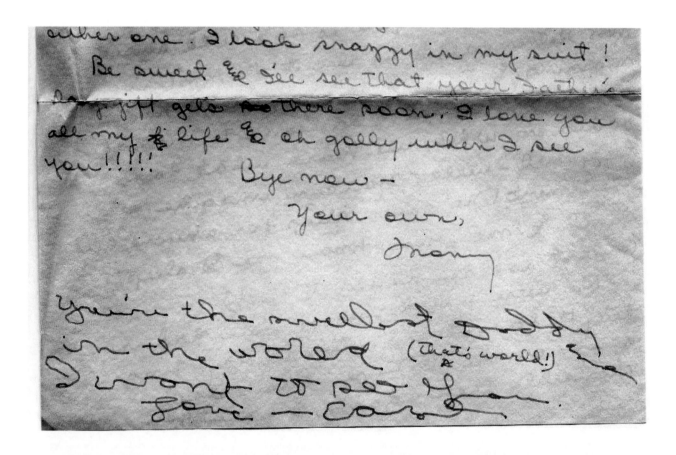

June 8, 1944 – from Ann, Newgulf, TX, to 3512 Ninth St., N.E., Wash DC

Wednesday

Hiya, my love,

We're getting along as well as can be expected – considering our wait. I'm being <u>very</u> patient though, not that I know we'll be together soon – but at times I can't deny I'm a <u>trifle</u> impatient! (Not much, just a little.)

Oh me – There's not much news, other than the hay gathering of last p.m. and the doing up of more peaches today. This evening, Sis and I are going in to Wharton. I hope I can get your Papa's Day gift off when I'm there – I guess you do, too!

Honey, I can think of <u>nothing</u> except our being together again. I'm trying to finish this damn watermelon dress before Saturday and since it's jersey weave, it's hell to sew on. I've got a dilly of a headache right now. I guess too much sewing at night – but that's about the only time I can get in a couple of hours straight except when the mess takes her nap. She's sleeping right now but since it's nearly 4:00 and Pop's due home at 4:15, I'd better get my bath. (It's only 3:30!) That'll give me more time. Lorry just got out of the bathroom so since it's empty, I'd better get on with the job of bathing of body – so until tonight then, sweet – bye now.

10:30pm.

Hi again! We just finished eating and doing the dishes – can you imagine – at this hour!

Pop got home about four thirty but we didn't get to Wharton. Looks like Saturday will be the day when I get my popsy his Papa's Day gift. Hope you like it. Anyway, when Pop got home, Lorry, Bobbie King, and I went to Newgulf after the mail. No letter from my man but I have hopes of tomorrow! Lorry got another graduation gift. A lovely rose suede bag to match her flower and gloves Aunt Tennie gave her. It's beautiful. When Aunt Martha came two weeks ago, she brought a white purse (the third L. received!) and brought it back home with her. She must have just gotten it because I imagine that shade was pretty hard to match. I remember a very lovely bag and purse of pale pink that a boyfriend gave me way back in 1939 – or was it? I think he was my husband, don't you? Or rather husband-to-be. I was just thinking today of the gifts you've given me since we've been married. Honey, I'm a lucky girl to have such a swell and thoughtful husband. It's getting kinda hard waiting, but the moment when I can start telling you all these things will make up for every little lonesome moment.

You're off Saturday 8 a.m. until Sunday 12 p.m. Golly, honey, when I think of this past weekend when we could have had so much time together. I'll be thinking of you this weekend and especially Sunday – Your Day. Your two girls will be with you before long and we'll declare a special Mother's and Father's Day (with Baby's Day thrown in for good measure!)

It's late and I could sleep on tacks tonight so I'm saying bye now. Keep yourself happy with the thought of our coming happiness as I'm doing. Be sweet for your two girls and write <u>soon</u>. I'll find out about the train fare when I get to Houston and will let you know. I'm coming out pretty good on my budget. We'll pour over it when I see you (oh joy!)

I love you all my life and I want to see you so bad.

Forever yours,

Mommy

June 9, 1944 – from Ann, Newgulf, TX, to 3512 Ninth St., N.E., Wash DC

Thursday p.m.
June 8, 1944

Dearest,

Received your letter of June 4 telling me of your weekend. Well, my friend, I <u>know</u> I'm coming now! Fine stuff – but really, honey, I'm glad you have friends up there. You know me, I'd die up there without friends (I'd be happy, tho, with just my lover.)

When I get back to Houston I'll find out about the train fare and about selling the car. Theo will help me and I know I'll get the best price.

I wish you'd answer my questions about where we're going to live and all about your actions. I'll probably go back to H (*Houston*) by the middle of the week and if I knew what to do I could go ahead with my plans. I know you're ready for us, but I still don't know how we're going to be taken care of. I'm thrilled about your extra allowance and am awaiting the $25.00 eagerly – it might get me half way to you! (oh, brother!) I'm also tickled about your Saturday night off. Golly, I can't do a very good job of waiting, sweet, so you'd better hurry up and send for your two girls!

The cat had kittens and they're so cute. Lorry brought one of them to Carol and she felt it and said "Da, Da" – so honey, you'd better start shaving a little closer! She was so cute with it. She patted it and hugged it but was gentle and didn't try to squeeze it at all! She let it climb all over her. Sweet little mess!

That damn watermelon dress - if you don't just fall out when you see it (because it's so beautiful), I'll pass out – I've worked so hard on it and had so many interruptions on it that I don't even know whether I'm even going to like it or not. But when I see you I'll probably be looking through rose colored glasses and maybe <u>I'll</u> even like the darn thing!

Enough about my woes now for a little straight stuff – There's not any news around here. Mom works like a Trojan and is still at it. She's snapping beans to can tomorrow. I'd be helping her if I had written you this evening – but there was that damn watermelon and I had to sew on it!

Where do you work? What building? Where do you live? Is the street address you gave me where you live or work? From one of your letters, I thought you were in the Pentagon but from your letter today I know you're not. Is it the State Dept Building? That's the one that houses the War Dept. I know so little about Wash (*Washington*). You've really got a job on your hands educating your dumb wife about D.C. (golly – I can hardly wait – hurry, hurry, you're missing plenty – woo woo!!!)

Honey, the wear and tear of cigarettes on my pocket book have given me an idea. I'm going to try to find one of those machines and roll my own. Yours too – when I get to D.C. That will help save quite a bit of extra money – and I don't think it's a bad idea anyway – how about you? I've smoked more since you've been gone and (before, too), so I think if I smoke home-made ones, I might cut down. Remember on our trip with Tommie and Norma? I didn't smoke much at all after we got back. I've cut down some since I've been here. For two whole days I had just about three all day, then that was when Pop got home. I didn't smoke cause I didn't have any. I've been out all day and smoked, well, this is my fifth – the first three were Bugler's – oh boy – are they rotten!

I'm going to quit now, sweet. Mom is almost through but I can help her finish up anyway so 'til tomorrow nite, I'll say again –

I love you all my life,

Yours,

Mommy

June 10, 1944 – from Ann in Newgulf, TX

Friday p.m.

Hello sweetheart,

Just put the chick to bed. It's eight o'clock and Lorry and I are going to the show in Boling just as soon as Mom gets through feeding. I hate to leave the baby in the house without someone here, so if I dash off in the middle of this you'll know what happened.

I'm still dying to hear about your Tuesday night rather Monday night – D-Day. I hope you wrote, if you did I should get it by tomorrow that is – unless you mailed it plain mail. I'm still out of Air Mails and 2 cents so this will have to go reg. again. We're going in to Wharton tomorrow and I'll get some then so tomorrow night your letter will be sent Air Mail. You'll get it, tho, before you get this one so <u>what am I talking for!!</u>

Still the same old stuff. Sammie Lou and Mrs. Franks came over today and Carol rushed into the living room about five minutes after they got here and came back with your picture just yelling "Da Da" and gave it to Mrs. F. It was precious.

By the way, Sammie Lou is engaged to a boy down at Camp Hulen – Ray Owens. They haven't made definite plans but I doubt if there'll be a whole lot of time passed now.

Kenneth King is due home sometime this week. He's bringing his wife with him. They're expecting a blessed event come August. They were married last August. They haven't wasted any time, have they?

Have you let the bunch at 1620 Main in on your activities. I hope so cause I wrote Joe last week and told him you had a job with the War Dept in D.C. but other than that I knew nothing at the time.

I'm getting kinda anxious to get back to Houston to get the ball rolling. I'm going to make a point of keeping all my clothes ready to ship within a few hours of receipt of a go wire. I'm also going to sell the car during the first few days after I get back. I also want to find out the cost and do several little things before I start packing. Just as soon as you get a place for us, wire or write Air Mail so I can express my things up. I'm going to take one bag on the train so I can just have a change for me and several things for the baby, including food for a few days just in case a diner is something in a dream! But don't forget, let me know the address – if I don't know it when I get your word, I'll just send it to 3512 9th St., NE in DC (what an address!)

Mom is just about through so I'm going to close now and hope for a letter tomorrow! Be sweet and remember – I miss you so much and get panicky when I think of this falling through – so pray, sweet, pray.

I love you all my life,

Yours always,

Mommy

June 13, 1944 – from Ann in Newgulf, TX

Saturday p.m.

Hello darling,

It's late, so I'll just say "I love you all my life" and say Goodnite.

Sunday 3pm

Hi Sweetheart,

Lorry wanted to go to the U.S.O. last night and we didn't get home until about 1:00, so that's why I didn't write when we came home. Bobbie didn't go because Kenneth and his wife came in and Lorry was supposed to be there 'cause she had invited a boy up from Camp Helen so Pop said if I'd go she could go. I didn't have the heart to say no, so I took her. I dropped her at the U.S.O. and went to the picture show all by my lonesome. It surely made me want to touch your hand or feel your arm around me. Anyway, I got out of the show about 20 min. to twelve. When I picked Lorry up, she and Eddie and I went over to the "Duck-Inn" and had an orange soda. I was slightly on the tired side when I got home, but I enjoyed it anyway.

We had quite a full day yesterday. We went in to Wharton when Pop came home and did a little shopping. I want you to write as soon as you get what I sent you yesterday. If you'd rather have something else, on the same line or something I can always get a refund on it. Let me know. If they don't fit, I'll return them and I'll buy you another when I get there (oh boy!).

We also did something else in Wharton. We took our little chicken to the doctor to have her final check-up. She's all well now and out of danger and no need for worry so now I can tell you all about it. We arrived here on Wednesday two weeks ago last Wed. and she was alright. When we took Aunt Martha home that Sunday and put her to bed, she seemed to be alright other than being slightly constipated. (I had given her castor on Sat. nite and that had been relieved.) She hadn't eaten well Sunday at noon.

Anyway, when she woke up from her nap, I knew she had a fever but there was no thermometer so I didn't tell anyone. (By the way, if you're wondering what Carol had – it was measles!) However, I'm straying from my story. We got back so late Sunday nite and she was sleeping so well I didn't disturb her until morning when I took her temperature. She had 102 (degrees). I gave her aspirin and called the new hospital in Wharton and made an appointment. When Pop got home, we whizzed over and when we got there, the chicken had 103 (degrees). Dr. Blassingame told us it would be at least ten or fifteen minutes before he could take care of us, so asked us if we minded if Dr. Blair would take her. I thought that was nice of him, so Dr. Blair became her official M.D. from then on. He went to school with Dr. Gardner and knows Dr. Wallis and Dr. Callaway, so he's OK as far as I'm concerned. Anyway, he said it looked like measles but the symptoms were still pretty much in the dark. He gave her some medicine and told us to keep her watched closely and let him know. Well, by the next afternoon, her fever had gone down to 101 (degrees) and she was still in excellent spirits. But by the time Pop came home the next afternoon (which was Wednesday) her fever had gone up to 104 2/5 (degrees)! Scared the living daylights out of us! We took her in and he gave her the most complete examination since she was born – even taking blood tests and a urinology among others. He's pretty thorough and naturally that made me feel pretty good. She started breaking out late Thursday evening and the fever vanished and hasn't returned yet. She was sleepy for two days and slept for those two days straight. The rest of the time was spent drinking Cokes, water, eating applesauce and pears and prunes. She started running off –rather her bowls did – the beginning of the second week. I started giving her broths with rice or chicken or noodles and that fixed her up. She has really been good, though. She started clearing up Thursday and by yesterday had cleared. The doctor said she's ok now. She's outside in the chicken yard with Pop and Mom right now and is so thrilled because she can get out. We had to put blankets over the shades because they let in too much light and there was a terrific track made from the bedroom to the "Do-Do" room. Every few minutes it was yelling "Mama – Mama – Do-Do". She just came to the window and she's so happy to be outside.

I'm going to quit now, sweet, because Lorry and I want to sew. I'll finish this tonight and tell you what your letters meant to me at this time. I love you.

10:20pm

After I finished the above, Lorry and I cut out the tops to some shorts. She's just finishing the bottom of hers and I finished mine earlier because I'm going to sew the shorts to the waist. The O.P.A. might not like it if I display my tires. They're not registered – you know!

I'll tell you all about how much your letters meant to me during the chicken's illness tomorrow. At this rate, that will be all I'll have to tell you tomorrow. I did want to tell you I received your Air Mail of the ninth today (the 11th) early this morning after church. I went by the Post Office and I was very thrilled at receiving it. It's so good to get a letter from you because just before I open them I have a very peculiar feeling that maybe this is the one that says "Come on!" I'm glad you're starting to look. I do wish, however, you'd look up May Quattlebaum. Aunt Tennie sent her address – it's 1332 Massachusetts Ave – Office of the Auditor, Tax Dept. She didn't know what building and I don't know her residence but I do wish you'd call on her. Try the directory for good measure. She may be able to pull a few strings.

I'm going now so be good and I love you all my life.

Yours forever,

Mommy

On a separate sheet of paper, Ann makes a record of Carol's illness that she refers to in the above letter:

Sunday, May 28 –	5:00pm, 102 deg.
Monday, May 29 –	7:30pm, 101 4/5 deg.
	9:00pm, 102 3/8 deg.
	10:30pm, 103 deg.
	Took to Dr. R.K. Blair, Wharton, Texas
Tuesday, May 30 -	7:30am, 100 4/5 deg.
	1:00pm, 102 deg.
	5:30pm, 104 2/5 deg.
	Dr. R.K. Blair prescribed aspirin and phenol barbatol
Wednesday, May 31 -	101 deg, highest temperature
Thursday, June 1 -	101 deg., highest temperature, eruption started
Friday, June 2 –	100 deg., highest

Past three days treatments included:
1/2 grain aspirin, 1/2 cpo
Cough syrup which was not given until eruption started. Then aspiring and cough syrup were given every four hours, when measles appeared

Saturday, June 3 –	9:30 – normal, the back of the neck seems to be drying up
Sunday, June 4 -	Free of fever all day – coughed more than usual (deep and loose)
	Bowels nearing normal. 2 b.m.s today. Began clearance of throat and

stomach.
Monday, June 5 -	5:00am, normal
	Stomach and throat, back and nape of neck clearing completely

---

June 14, 1944 – from Ann in Newgulf, TX

Tuesday a.m.
June 13, 1944

My sweetheart,

I missed last p.m. because a boyfriend of Lorry's came down from Camp Helen and spent the day. Right after supper, we took him to Newgulf and showed him around the field. We took him to the vats, the reservoir, and the sulphur blocks. He was so impressed it was funny! We got back here about 10:00 and then took him to Wharton to catch the bus at 12:00. We had about an hour and a half to kill so we went to the U.S.O. and danced. I danced with him! First time I've danced since you left – oh no – Bobbie's dance was the first time, wasn't it? Anyway, Bobbie and I were together and he'd dance with us out of politeness, I'm sure. There were a few other soldiers there but they were playing ping-pong. One guy was sitting alone and he came over to talk with Bobbie and me. He was about 35 (or older) and had been in North Africa. He went over after prisoners and brought them back on a prison ship. He's a mess sergeant at the Wartou P.O.W. Camp. He was interesting but couldn't dance so B (*Bobbie*) lost interest pretty quick. I talked with him until he left – about 11:45, and went to the "Duck Inn" where an M.P. came in and told us they weren't allowed to serve drinks to service men after 11:30. We left and went to the station and sat there until 20 min. to 1:00. At 12:00, I said you were just starting to work and then I thought of the difference in time and decided you'd been at work an hour already. We had a real nice time.

Pop forgot to mail your letter yesterday so we mailed it last nite. It's the long Air Mail that tells all. Hope you've already received it cause I sent May Quattlebaum's address in it.

Golly, it would be swell to get a letter this evening saying you'd found an apartment or room or something that would take care of us. Take anything you can find, cause I have a strong feeling it'll be long enough as it is.

Lorry's washing dishes so I'll close and go help her. I want to put this in the King's mailbox so the Postman can pick it up around 1:00.

Oh, I did want to tell you this. Our chicken milked a cow this morning! She was just pulling the tits for all she was worth. After the milking was over, she helped Mom pick cucumbers and was a dirty little mess, but a very happy one! I'll tell you all about a lot of things when I see you.

I believe I'm going home Sat or Sun, maybe before. Anyway, I'll get everything settled and if you haven't found anything in a couple of weeks, I'll come back and spend another week with them here. I've really enjoyed myself, and I don't think it'll be easy to forget how swell they've been to me.

I'll go now cause if I don't hurry, Lorry will be drying them herself. So by now – I love you all my life.

Your anxious spouse,

O.A.O.

P.S.: I still think I'm dreaming! Love you - Mommy

June 14, 1944 – from Ann in Newgulf, TX

Wednesday
June 14, '44

Hi sweetheart,

There's still no news, except the baby got into Lorry's stationery and tore two three-cent stamps to bits. It tried to pay her back but she said to put it on your letter tonite so that's why I'm sending this piece of nothing Air Mail.

Carol helped around the place all day. We missed her and turned around to see her coming out of the garage with a screw driver in her hand – she headed straight for the little tractor and decided that wasn't what was needed. (All this time she didn't know we were watching her.) She went back into the garage and came out this time with a bolt – headed for the tractor and placed it in a little hole! Mom said if she were a boy, she'd be really Wm III! She was so cute. Lorry and I have been sewing all day and when Mom was outside so was she. Mom doesn't like for her to be out alone but she and Mopsy go all over the place whenever the opportunity arises. Today she was outside alone and (usually the cats follow her, too) she decided she had to come in – well, the cat was on the walls and she couldn't get around him – she kept yelling "Move, Move!" and he'd zig and she would. She'd zag and he would – it was a scream – she finally yelled "Mommy – I want Mommy – Move – Move – I want Mommy". She wasn't crying – she was just mad at the cat and telling him she wanted her mommy. Mom and I were watching and nearly in hysterics when she hit the steps and both Mopsy and the cat and Carol were all crawling up when she (the chicken) met and then yelled "Mama-do-do". Since it was too late anyway, we just stood there and watched to see what she'd do next. She turned to the cat and pointed down at her feet and said "See – do-do" – We really yelled!

I guess that's about all for today's Diary. I wish I'd hear a little more from you. All I need is a bedroom. Leave the rest until I get there. We can manage, sweetheart. I don't care what it is. Just don't forget to wire the <u>minute</u> you find something and include the address so I can express any extra baggage. If we need anything else, except clothes, include that too, in the telegram.

I'm going to Houston Sunday. We may go Saturday, I'm not sure, but if you find a place Saturday, wire Houston – if Sunday and from then on, wire Houston.

I'll go now, sweet, so be good (I mean it – don't do any straying – by the way, why did you leave when the girl's husband came home and did you have dinner with them Sunday – what kind are they? – do you like them?)

Bye now –

I love you all my life and I miss you so much – please hurry –

Love you,

Mommy

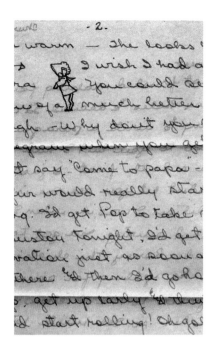

Copy of June 16 letter with Ann's drawing of Carol

June 16, 1944 – from Ann in Newgulf, TX

Thursday

Hi sweet,

Just finished making four button holes and decided I'd quit sewing and write a paragraph or two to you but I had to take a bath first. I just couldn't let you see me in the condition I was in when I finished sewing. I've got to go outside, honey. The chick's out there and yelling for someone to go out to the chicken yard with her so I'll write later. Bye now – love you.

Ha – she changed her mind and came in. It's so hot out there and she has a seersucker jacket and bonnet on so I guess she's rather warm – she looks like this. (Ann drew a picture of Carol's profile in the outfit). I wish I had a camera so you could see her. I know of a much better way though – why don't you send me a telegram when you get this and just say "Come to papa" – I'll bet fur would really start flying. I'd get Pop to take me to Houston tonight. I'd get a reservation just as soon as I got there and then I'd go home, sleep, get up early and things would start rolling! Oh golly – I hope it won't be too long before you find some little vacant hole somewhere!

10p.m. – Lorry and I just got back from Boling. We went to the show there and saw "The Hour Before Dawn". It was a war picture and I didn't enjoy it as much as I would have a comedy or musical, but I've been sewing for four days straight without getting out once so thought the movies might relax the old lady. It did, too.

Squirt has really enjoyed herself today. After Pop came home, he took her back about 10 acres and he was really puffing and blowing – but she was in high spirits indeed! She's Miss Fixit DeLuxe and also the greatest bare back rider in this county! She rides Mike every day (he's the pretty little bully out back), and wants to "ride" every time she sees anyone going outside.

Pop just woke up (he was lying here on the sun porch) and said to tell you to find a place just for me – that they would take care of her – I can sure laugh loud! Mom heard it and yelled from the bedroom – "That's not so good, is it?" What do you think about it?

I got a buyer for the car. A friend of Pop's wants it for his daughter-in-law. I'm going to get prices in Houston, then if he can top my best offer, I'm going to sell it to him. How much do you think I ought to get – or do you have any idea? I'm going to get Theo to go around with me to get prices on it. I'll keep you posted and if there's anything you don't like, you can let me know by an Air Mail Special Delivery. I'll quit now and go do-do – Bye now.

I love you all my life,

Mommy

June 17, 1944 – from Ann, Newgulf, TX

Friday

Hello sweetheart,

Received your letter and was so thrilled with it. If that's a "quick" one, how about a few more like it? It really made me feel swell! No kidding.

Honey, if, as you say, we could get a room there at 3512 – why not let me go ahead and make my reservations – then I'll be sure of having at least a seat all the way. From the talk around here, it looks like it'll be ten-day wait for through reservations. If I went ahead and came on a certain day, and you hadn't found a place yet, I'd be tickled with one room with a shared bath and kitchen. I really mean it, sweet. I can be happy <u>anywhere</u> with you. Remember, I've told you that ever since you first asked me whether I'd like living away from H. (*Houston*) when you were thinking about the possibilities of being transferred. See!

Honey, Robert and Bernadine Wynn are there in D.C. Jiggs came over and said he's lost track but I wanted to go by Mrs. Wynn's and find out for sure but the baby being sick has really thrown our party. Ralph Robinson is there, too. Wouldn't that be swell if Bob and Bernie were there?

I've got so many things to tell you that I'll <u>never</u> quit talking (except when you're kissing me)! There are so many things about the chicken that will <u>amaze</u> you when you see her. She's so sweet and has grown so much. She talks about you all the time – Da-Da – so sweet!

Pop is taking the clock – at last. I guess you were beginning to wonder about it, but he's forgotten it every morning. He's afraid you'll be late for work after what you said in your letter so I don't think he'll forget it in the morning.

Honey, we're going to Houston Sunday so from now on be sure to address all letters to 1203.

I hope you like my wardrobe. I've been doing quite a bit of sewing lately. Besides a few things of the baby's I've made one nice dress, one three piece (no, two piece – the shorts are one), playsuit, two house dresses for me. I want to do a little more before I go to you because if I can't find a friend with a machine, these will have to do me quite awhile (I hope!).

Say, lover, have you received our Father's Day gifts? Be sure and let me know cause they were insured. I imagine you've already received them though.

I'm going to quit now. It's a few minutes to eleven (you're just starting for work!) – (I'll bet you're already there tho cause it's about 3 min to 12 there). Golly – but I want to see you.

I think you're a pretty swell guy yourself, sweetheart – so remember I love you all my life and can hardly wait to see you – bye now –

Yours,

Mommy

P.S.: Pretty swell about the Japan Mainland bombing, eh? Four planes and 5 men lost. Poor people whose boys there were, but I think it's swell no more were lost, don't you? Bye again - I love you, Mommy

---

June 17, 1944 – from Ann in Newgulf, TX

Saturday p.m.
6/17/44

Hi sweet,

I got that letter today that I've been waiting for so long! I'll wire you when my reservations are made. We'll be in Houston tomorrow so I can get right at it. I'm going to get Theo to help me sell the car just as soon as he can do it. I've got all my clothes and the baby's all clean and ready to go. You know how I feel about the one – room business. You've heard nothing but that for the letters of the past week! Oh, honey, I was so happy when I got that letter that I felt like all I had to do was grab the chicken, take a good running start and take off and fly to Wash(*ington*)!

Oh, yes, I wanted to tell you about Pete Serrill from Newgulf. He (Pop) said you'd remember him. He's the brother of the man who took you to the hospital when you cut your arm. Anyway, he's a White House Guard. He stands right in front of it. Now it may be he's in front of the capitol – you know Pop!

Honey, do you think I ought to bring cooking utensils, knives and forks and dishes or do you think we can send for these things when we get the apt? Let me know cause if you think we'll need these things, I can express them the same time I send my luggage. I'm going to carry one suitcase with changes for as many days as we're going to be on the train. Then I can put the baby's food in it too and it won't be hard keeping up with it. Don't you think that is the best idea?

I want to tell you so many things about Carol but I'd be writing until midnite (that's only about 30 min from now). You've already been on the job that long! I'll go now and save all those things when we meet again.

I love you all my life –

Your Mommy

June 19, 1944 – from Ann, back in Houston, at her parents' house, 1203 Missouri Ave.

Sunday p.m.
June 18, 1944

Hello sweetheart,

Well, here I am writing with Lorry's pen again. That 35¢ pen of mine hasn't given me good service at all! Only two years of constant wear and tear!

We arrived here this evening just after three. We had a nice trip but it was hot as the devil.

Now for what was waiting for me when I arrived! An Air Mail Special Delivery (of which I knew nothing), I'd waited so patiently for that telegram and <u>never</u> did receive it! We were home all day Saturday and from the postmark on the letter (June 17, 6pm), you must have sent the telegram before six at least. Anyway, it was news to me and I <u>can't</u> calm down! I've had a terrific headache ever since and I took a B.C. but all it did was ease it a little!

Aunt Tennie knows a guy who can get my reservations for me a whole lot sooner than anyone else. The ticket agent said a month but a fellow Pop knows can get one in ten days. But I'm sure the one Aunt Tennie knows can get it a lot sooner. She's going to find out first thing in the morning and will let me know. I'll Air Mail a letter to let you know. I'm going to get rid of the car tomorrow. I'm also going to the bank and deposit my checks. I'm going to get my statements fixed, but I have to take Lorry to the bus station in the morning and try to get her overnight case before I do. Hope I can get one that's not too expensive. I've got so darn much to do though I don't know how I'll ever do it all tomorrow. I'm going to get estimates on the car though and try to get it sold before the sun sets.

I've finished my dress and I won't do any more sewing – but you said if I had anything else to bring it and finish it up there – there doesn't happen to be a sewing machine around, does there?

Sweet, about the baby bed – It can be taken apart and shipped – wouldn't you feel better about it? I think I would. I appreciate the work the landlady (what's her name?) must have gone to, but it would be easy to ship the bed and mattress when I send my bags – what do you think?

I understand about meeting you. I'll wire and we can make plans better when we know what time I'll be in. I'll know by tomorrow so I'll write you as soon as I know anything definite. I will not destroy your letters! I want to read them all some rainy day when we're in our home in the post war world.

Sweetheart, I'm also going to put all of our insurance papers, birth certificates, et al, in the safety deposit box, too. Mama suggested this and I don't think it's a bad idea, do you?

By the way, our radio's on the bum again so I hate to ask Theo for his. They might want to get it fixed for themselves so keep trying to buy batteries.

I'm going to go now, sweet. I'll drop you a line sometime tomorrow. I hope it'll be early. You will probably receive these two pretty close together.

Good nite, sweet – I love you all my life.

Your Mommy

June 20, 1944 – from Ann in Houston

Monday p.m.

My darling,

I've had a lovely day today. I've had two offers for the car, but I couldn't get any estimates because the fluid is out of the brakes and since it's June tenth I couldn't get a nigger anywhere. I'll get that done tomorrow. I'm going to express the baby's bed, bed linen and toys Wednesday. I may be able to get it off tomorrow but I doubt it. I'll send my luggage at the same time if I send it Wednesday. You'll probably have a wire by now but anyway – when I received your wire I had to laugh! Honey – do you know that Aunt Tennie has been taking telegrams all day telling certain people there weren't and wouldn't be reservations for another 30 days! How do you like her being able to get them for me in four days! Just think, sweet, I'll be there Sunday morning. I'll be in the station about 5 something. I have to wait until morning to get my tickets so I'll wire then. I'm so thrilled I haven't got good sense. You're going to have the help me balance my checkbook. I can't find some dollars and cents – not much but enough to start me wondering. You'll die the way I've done it!

Hope I can say tomorrow that I've sold the car at a good price. I talked to Jean Conley, Dorothy and Peggy today. I want to go to the office with the baby before I leave. Dorothy told me that Van is stationed in Los Angeles and will be there for a year or 18 mos. at least. She's going to visit him in a month but I hope she can go sooner and stay with him. He's living on a subsistence salary off the post and works from 8 to 5 – off an hour every noon! I want to call Mrs. Norris tomorrow and find out about Norma and Tommie. Ralph called Mrs. K last night and I'm going to get her to give me his telephone number. He gave it to her so we can call him when I get there. I'll wire you in the morning, sweet, but I'm going to start taking your advice right away and go to bed early – it's always midnight before I get there so I'm going to take a powder and try 10:30 for a change.   Bye now.

I love you all my life –

See you Sunday!

Mommy

After the above letter, there are no other letters included in the batch from Spring 1944. Apparently, Ann and Bill communicated either via telegram or phone until meeting up with each other again on Sunday, June 23, 1944.

But letters continued to be sent!

Four Generations: George Friedrich Brandt and Julia Hickel Brandt, front right: their daughter Matilda Julia Wilhelmina Brandt Genzer and William Genzer, front left; their son William Adolf Genzer and Sarah Ann Quattlebaum Genzer, standing; and their baby daughter, Carol Ann, c. 1942.

Sept. 24, 1944 – from George Friedrich Brandt, Bill's maternal grandfather, RFD No 3, LaGrange, TX – mailed to Mrs. Wm Genzer, 1603 S. 28th St., Arlington, VA

As George's native language is German, many of the words that he writes in this letter are misspelled. So, I took the liberty of correcting as much as I could, but I did not alter the grammar.

La Grange Sep 24/44

Dear Children,

We was glad to hear from you, and hope the war be over by Christmas, so all of you be home so we celebrate our Golden Wedding dobbel (*?*) on Dec. 26, 1944.

We got a letter from Lawrence and wife. They expecting a great-grandson for us some time in October. Lawrence and his family be with us to celebrate.

Dear Ann, You been writing Bill taken up on Uncle Sam feed him got also Garel that is fine, but you, that puzzled me (shucks!). Should we expect the great-grandson at least. Hope to hear from you soon.

Your Grandparents

P.S.: Please let me know what class of soldier Bill is. G.F.B.

November 16, 1944 – from Wharton, TX (Willie and Tillie Genzer)

To: Sgt. and Mrs. William A. Genzer
1603 South 28th St.
Arlington, Virginia

At some point between June 1944 and November 1944, Bill was promoted from Private to Sergeant, but not sure when that occurred.

Matilda "Tillie" Genzer, Bill's mother is now 46 years old, as she just had a birthday.
Lawrence Edward Ripper (Tillie's sister Martha's second son) and his wife Winnifred have a new baby born on Oct. 21, 1944, named Annette Ripper.
Tillie also mentions Opa and Oma's (her parents, George Friedrich Brandt and Julia Hickel Brandt) as they are about to celebrate their 50th wedding anniversary coming up on December 26, 1944. George is 72 and Julia is 69.
Grandma Genzer refers to Agnes Anne Bach Knapik Genzer, 75 years old. Her husband, Joseph Genzer, Willie's father, died in 1925.

Dear Bill, Ann, and Carol,

Way down Washington, I know you are thinking why it is Mom don't send those things. But I am sending it now. Look like it took so long until I got things to gather. I hope you wasn't in need of them. I should of send them sooner already but you know how it is here. If you want some things you must let me know a month ahead of time so you get them when you need them.

I couldn't find my any sheets in that box where the pillow slips were in. So I am sending you two bought ones and what I made out of those sacks of mine. Sis called your mother and asked her if there are any of your sheets over there so your Mother said she would look in your boxes. That she had a box to send you and if they were, she would send them, and am sending Bill those handkerchiefs for his birthday and some for you too. And a dish cloth so you can wash dishes and a hot pad to hold hot dishes so you won't get burnt. (How do you like that?) And an apron to top it off. And for Sugar, a little house coat and a little bucket. And some pecans. If that all gets there alright I will send you all some more pecans. You let me know if you got it all alright.

Oh yes, I sent you six pillow slips and that pretty knife set. I couldn't find that knife you wanted. There are no big knives with the table knives and forks.

We got your letter yesterday and was glad to hear from you all and thank you all very much for the pretty birthday card. Pop opened the letter when he got it from the post office and started to read it and when came to where it said Carol was sick, he said he quit reading and came home and told me to read it. He said Carol is sick. You don't know how relieved we felt when I came to where it said she is alright again. You all be sure and take care of our sweet little girl. We are waiting for the time so we can get to see you all. I know Sugar is a big girl already. The folks out at Holman are getting things ready for the Golden Wedding and Opa and Oma are sure thinking that you all can come too, but I told them not to think about it too hard because we don't know if you all can be with us all. But of course, we all wish you all could be with us. Lawrence and Winnifred and their little girl they think they may be with us Christmas but they don't know for sure either if he get a furlough.   Their baby was born on Carol's birthday Oct 21, 1944.

By the way, Mrs. Staffa gave Pop an address to send to you, she said Rudolf and his wife are in Alexandria, VA. She asked for you all address and I gave it to them. But said they couldn't find you all, so she want you all to try and write or call she gave the phone number.

Grandma Genzer is sending hello to you all. Oh yes, she made the apron I sent you. And a sweet kiss to baby Carol.

Oh yes, I never did tell you George is staying with us, he is going to farm 110 acres of land from Jack Chatmann and is going to help us work our 20 acres with his tractor. So we won't be ourselves, since Sis left off to school. Of course she comes home every week and so far that helps so much.

You all be sweet and take care of yourselves. Love and kisses from

Mom and Pop

Write often if it is just one page.

Bill, Baby Ann, and little Carol Genzer in Virginia, c. 1944-45.

January 25, 1945 – from Carita Mauboules, on Benton W. Mauboules' stationary, Rayne, LA

To: Mrs. Bill Genzer
1603 South 28th St.
Arlington, Virginia

Wednesday
7:30 a.m.

Dear Baby Ann,

The first thing I want to tell you is that I certainly appreciate your letters. I know that must be hard to believe considering I never answer them but it's the truth. I made up my mind yesterday I'd write you and the day went by, and I hadn't. So this morning, before I do anything – here I am.

I am so happy all three of you are together and well. Needless to add – and happy. Your mother wrote me this week and said how Xmas without you all didn't seem just right. I haven't seen them since Labor Day. I had thought surely I'd go over after I got thru with my relief work in Jennings, but you know how it is sometime. I am waiting to go to Kaplan for a month. The operator over there hasn't seen her husband in 2 ½ years and expects him any day. I am getting tired waiting. I wish I had a permanent job. It's nice work, by very confirming. But, all work is that way.

Odette got a card from Grover Jr. Sunday and is so happy. Just a typewritten card but it's something after all these years. Mama is here since Tues. She is well. Melba and her family the same. The children are getting so big. Carita is bigger than Melba and such a nice child! I hope she stops growing. Robert is a Mouton. Lazy as hell. And Melba's pet. Just like Memere and Emile. In fact, even Melba has to admit it. Mignon is as big as Robert – almost – and can take care of herself. At present she and her teacher are having trouble. Melba is thinking of putting her in the convent – telling the teacher what she thinks of her – and several other things, that Mignon most probably tells the teacher. Anyway, she's punished regular and Melba can't stand that. But Minnie I am sure as Tom says, puts it on the teacher. So I don't know what will happen. Nothing won't probably – just talk from Memere. Life goes by just the same. I regret I can't see my folks as much as I would like to but I guess that's my cross! Sometime it gets heavy, but it could be worse.

Martha Lee and John were here during the holidays. He looks fine and she does to. They are in San Antonio with Hattie. He's lucky he's back in the states altogether. I will stop now – bring Mama coffee and finish later.

Liza is still here, but Bootsy quit me last May. So Liza has more to do, and spends most of her time fussing. Whiskey is fine. Spoiled terribly. I hope Carol is well. She must be big now. I would love to see her. Give Bill my love. Write me again sometime and even tho I am a first class heel about answering don't think it's because I don't think of you. You were always such a nice child – don't change. Well, it's time to stop.

Lots of love for you three,

Carita

February 5, 1945 – from Mrs. Louis D. Herring (Dottie), Violet Avenue, Poughkeepsie, New York

Feb. 4, 1945

Dear Anne,

It's needless for me to say I was overwhelmed by all the good news – your coming next Monday and the probabilities of an apartment near you. I hope you received the telegram OK.

When you hit dear ole Po'keepsie call me and we'll pick you up at the station – that is orders from headquarters.

I was so ticked over the news – I'm practically a nervous wreck. I'll have plenty of packing and planning to do know. The family feels pretty bad about our leaving – not so much over me as over Dougie I think. I think we'll make out OK though. (*Letter is ripped, so some content is missing here.*)

Anne, I can't wait till next Monday. We'll really have plenty to talk over now. Maybe we'll all be going back to Wash together if things work out alright.

Dougie and I are just about over our colds. The past week has really been miserable – you better get ready for some cold weather and I'm not kidding.

Does Bill think he'll be able to get a 3-day pass? Lou's had several already so I don't know about him. He'll be able to get home for a day anyway – Bill probably can get the three days. I hope so anyway.

Well pal – I'll say so long now til Monday – the 12th – have a nice trip.

Regards to Bill and kiss Carol for Doug and I.

Love,

Dottie

Feb. 7, 1945 – from Tillie Genzer in Newgulf, TX

To: Sgt. and Mrs. William A. Genzer
1603 South 28th St.
Arlington, Virginia

Wed. Feb. 7, 1945

Dearest Children,

I know you think we have forgotten about you all, but we didn't. Because I didn't write in a long time. But we are always looking for a letter from you. But I promise I will write oftener.

Lawrence and wife and baby are at home now and will leave Friday again. Their baby sure is precious, it is so big and active and not afraid of no one. We were at the Rippers last Friday night to see them. Then Saturday, Lawrence and family went to her people and Martha and Gus came out here and spent Saturday night and Sunday and left Monday morning.

I had a dinner Saturday night for George and his girlfriend so she met George's folks we had a nice time we played bridge and tarocks, we were eight of us, George and his girl Sis and Ralph, Martha and Gus and Pop and I. I think George really like it staying here with us. He found him this girl up at the Triple A office you see is working for the Triple A. On his spare time, when he cannot work in the field, he is working 135 acres.

He is moving his negro family down here, he had working for him at Uncle Willie's. We are hoping he will do good here he has got some good land rented.

Pop is on his vacation now for 2 weeks he started Monday the 5th and will be off until the 19th. But he is working more than he would be on the job.

He is helping George to fix the house for the negros. He went after some time to fix the roof yesterday and got 14 sacks of potatoes for planting for us. We are going to plant about 3 acres of potatoes in about 3 weeks.

Since George is going to have those negros here, they are going to help us too. They are 12 in the family and 8 or 9 what can work.

Did you all get the box we sent you about 4 weeks ago? I hope you did. And Sis said she didn't hear from you if you got her big picture she sent you all. She sent it before Xmas. I guess you got the carcages (?)and cake and pictures Ore Nell sent you from the Golden Wedding.

Well I promise I will write in a few days again. I know our little Sugar is getting so big we won't know her when we see again look you all are gone so long but hope and pray it won't take so long anymore so you all can come home soon.

Love and kisses from us all,

Mom, Pop and George

On Monday, February 12, 1945, Ann took Carol up to Poughkeepsie, NY, by train for a period of time. Apparently, they are staying with Louis and Dottie Herring. The below letters are from that time. Carol is now 2 years 4 months old.

Feb. 14, 1945 – from Ann in Poughkeepsie, NY, to Bill at 1603 S. 28th St., Arlington, VA

Ann used Dottie Herring's stationery to write this letter to Bill. Ann references that she is pregnant with their second child, who will be born in October 1945, William Robert Genzer. She is about two months pregnant at the time.

Tuesday a.m.

Hello Sweetheart,

Couldn't write last nite as Carol was a bit upset and didn't want me to leave her. She's OK today, however, and I think she'll be alright from now on as she becomes more familiar with everything.

I already miss you. In fact, I started missing you when you got off the train. Carol was a doll all the way – I couldn't have asked her to be any better. She sat in her seat and played with a little sailor doll a little boy gave her. His name was Wickie so Carol calls the little doll "Wickie" and loves it. When we got to Penn Station I caught a cab for Grand Central. I had about 45 minutes to wait, but thought I'd find out what track my train was on so when we got through eating we'd get right on the train and not lose any time. Boy, were we lucky – the train left at 3:57 instead of 4:15 and I got right on it with about 10 minutes to spare! Didn't get anything to eat but got a sandwich and milk after we got on the train. We really made grand connections, but I'm still glad I inquired before eating or would have had to wait two hours for another train!

The snow is terrific – the ride up here is beautiful – the Hudson is completely frozen over – ice and snow everywhere – really lovely.

Tell all the kids hi for me and will drop Rita a note sometime today.

Carol is having the time of her life going up and down the stairs. Everyone up here has had a fit over her. They can't get over her hair. Say she's beautiful – you should be proud of our baby!

I'm still OK. Nary a sign of my country cousin! Oh boy – told Dottie – she thought I was kidding, but once I convinced here she's as thrilled as we are about it!

Will run now – forgive the short scribbled note but will do better later.

I love you and miss you –

Yours,

Preggy

P.S.: You're my Valentine, you know!

February 15, 1945 – from Ann in Poughkeepsie, NY

Louis and Dottie Herring appear to be family friends. Louis has a sister named Dot, not to be confused with his wife Dottie. Wow!

Wednesday
Feb 14, 1945

Hello Sweetheart,

Dottie and I just got back from the show. Made me very homesick for you. I'd sure like to kiss you – oh boy! By the way, Happy Valentines Day!

Say, I still haven't received those goulashes. I really need them too – snow is really deep and I'm so thrilled with this place – it's truly beautiful – but please Popsy, come for me next weekend. I can stand this weekend without you but not another, so let me know when you're coming. We'll leave here so we can have a day together before you have to go back to work.

Sweet, you should see Carol in the snow! She adores it. We took the kids sleigh riding yesterday and - well, I'll tell you all about it in another letter or in person. Nick took us riding today. Really saw "Keepies" – It's going to knock your eyes out, it has mine popping now!

Met Dot – Lou's sister – the one they say I remind them of – well, it's really a compliment – she's really darling. Dottie and I had a drink with her before we went to the show. She reminds me of Lou – has that grand personality. She's having a party tomorrow nite – spaghetti supper. We're going and will probably meet Lou's mother then. If she's half as charming as her son and daughter – well, that's that! The people up here remind me so much of your family – all the aunts are like Aunt Martha – perfectly swell. Aunt Anna made two pairs of riding breeches for Carol – a blue (sky blue at that!) and a brown one. She looks like a dream!

Well, sweet, guess this is all for now – make those plans now as I miss you terrifically. Give a big hug to yourself and kiss your pillow –

I love you all my life –

Your Mommy

(Ann included a lipstick kiss at the bottom of the letter.)

February 15, 1945 – from Ann in Poughkeepsie, NY

Thursday
Feb. 15, 1945

Hello, my Daddy,

Gee, it was swell to hear your voice – really made me homesick. You can do that again – but not on Sat. nite – I might start howling. When do you think I'll outgrow that? Sweet, it might be a better idea if you go ahead and come with Lou. Then Sat morn, you can go home and get some rest and have company on the way here too. Dottie was talking to me and I was so happy I didn't know what I was saying! Hope we can go home Monday morning, tho, as I want a little time with you at home – so tell everybody when you get here that Rita and Andre are meeting us at the train and that's that – How about it?

The baby has a rough cold but so far no fever. I ran the inhalator, gave her cough medicine and aspirin all day. Gave her milk of magnesia last nite, so her bowels are on. I told her you called and she just smiled and went back to sleep! We sure do miss you, old man, and although I'm having a swell time, wish I were home! But to get back to Carol – damn drafty brains! I know that's what gave her the cold. No sir – no more trips during winter – don't care that much for travelling. (So don't get a furlough til summer!!!) I'm going to really dress her for the trip back home.

Hope everything's OK. What did you do tonite? There were so many things I wanted to ask you and I didn't say a thing! Did I get any mail – hope you forwarded it. I know I didn't want you to but I can just imagine how swell mail would make me feel these a.m.'s! I'm sitting on the Johnny that's why this is unusually bad! I'm really sleepy – had a bottle of beer and I'm ready to pass out! We played Pinochle after you called. I guess that's about all, sweet, for tonite. Write me – you lug!

I love you, and as for a Valentine – you gave that to me when you gave me your name – I love you all my life. Good nite, sweet, sleep tite and I'm taking good care of <u>both</u> your children.

Your ever loving Mommy

February 17, 1945

This letter is from Mrs. Theo Frank Jr., Bellaire, TX (Ann's older sister, Bobbie), to Mrs. W.A. Genzer, 1603 S. 28th St., Arlington, VA

Bobbie is currently 26 years old, her husband Theo is 29. Their daughters are Roberta Dianne, 5, and Susan Elise, 3. Mother is Ann and Bobbie's mother, Sarah Ann Mouton Quattlebaum, 52 years old.

Friday

Dear all,

You had better sit down before you fall down. I have started a hundred times to write and, well, you know how it is. But I promise I won't wait so long to write from now on.

There isn't much news. Dianne has had a cold for weeks. Can't seem to get rid of it, but on the whole everyone is fine.

We haven't had any winter at all yet. It has been warm enough to go without coats, just like summer for the past week.

Theo is playing poker tonight so we had dinner at Mother's. I am writing this while I am here cause I know if I wait until I get home, I'll put it off again. Isn't that terrible?

We haven't been doing a thing. We haven't been out in so long, that is, to do anything exciting, I wouldn't know how to act. Lillie and Bruce are building a barbecue pit in the back yard so they work on it every spare moment. We really are going to enjoy it this summer.

I have been riding horseback with my husband lately. I bought boots, riding pants, shirt, and belt. Can you imagine that? It really is a lot of fun and I am getting real good, too.

I am writing this on your desk and looking right at Carol's picture and wishing so that I could see her and you both. When do you think you can come home on furlough? Wish so much that you could.

Mother is sewing on Carol's Easter dress. It is adorable. She said to tell you she is sending a box. It's for Valentine's. She said it would be later but better late than never.

You asked in your letter to tell you about the girl at Dianne's birthday party. Her name was Lillian Teachworth. A loudmouth! I am sure you know all about how she acted so won't go into it. I practically had to insult her. But you asked about her name so thought I would tell you.

Dorys Reed has moved to Dayton, Ohio, so thought I would tell you so you would know why you haven't heard from her.

Mother wants to take me home before it gets too late so better close. Write soon and kiss my baby for me.

Love,

Bobbie

February 17, 1945 – from Ann in Poughkeepsie, NY

Friday, Feb. 16, 1945

My darling -

Knew you'd be worried about the baby. She's fine. Was going to call but couldn't find your number. I guess I left it at home. Anyway – no fever and I doctored her up again tonite. She'll be alright tomorrow – thank goodness! Thought for awhile there we were going to have that 105° business again, but I guess I caught it in time, thank heaven.

Played pichonicle (sp!!!!) with Nick and Mary and Dot. Really like them. Lou's mother spent the afternoon with us. She's swell – looks so much and reminds me so much of Aunt Hattie. I really feel at home around this place – with so many of them looking like our folks. Lou's mother is just as cute as I thought she'd be. Perfectly swell, too. Carol really went for her – from the very first, too.

Dot and I may go to town tomorrow. Hope I can get some clothes. If you see a cute blond in a blouse that I'd like – snatch it – the blouse – not the blond!!! I guess Jr. is really on the way. I had sort of a brown discharge today and it scared me. Thought I was getting the curse. I've been feeling too swell to be pregnant, too, but think maybe we hit it this time. Hope so!

Guess I'll run up and take my bath and put the body to bed. Carol kept me up practically all nite. She called out about every hour to be put on the pot – then wouldn't go. I was out today – but you know me, just as soon as the sun goes down, I start perking up!

Take it easy – am counting the days til I see my old man – really miss you, punk – kiss yourself in the mirror for me and tell Rita and Andre we'll either be in at 6 or 8 Monday nite, the 26th. We'll let you know after consulting the time table – Dot says hi –

I love you.

Yours,

Preggy

February 18, 1945 – from Ann in Poughkeepsie, NY

Saturday
Feb. 17, 1944 (*sic*)

Dearest one,

Jiminy, I miss you. Can't wait for next weekend. If I go any place without you again – please don't make me stay any more than <u>one</u> week. That's plenty for anyone's visit – especially mine.

Dot and I are going to town this afternoon. I feel groggy as hell in this place. It's so damn hot here, I don't want you ever talking (or me, either) about Mama's house! My room is the coolest in the house – that's not cold either. No windows open, even at nite. The first nite I didn't sleep and woke up feeling groggy. Maybe if we got out more it would be better. I know that's another reason the baby caught cold. Dot's asleep or I'd never write like this – but she knows it anyway.

Carol's writing you a letter too. We both miss you. Will be so glad when next Sat comes! Oh joy – it'll be wonderful to talk to someone. I know I blow off to only you – I can't talk with anyone the way I do you – Guess that's why we're so much closer than most couples. Hope I can find a skirt and a couple of blouses. I don't have a thing, but I hate to buy a lot of stuff if I'm pregnant – which I'm pretty sure of now – Gee, I come around now – you'll see one disappointed little gal!

Wrote Mama and Daddy and Pop and Mom last nite, too. I know they'll like it.

Well, babe, I feel better now that I've blown off a little steam. I'll be so glad to see you. It'll be swell going home together on the train – won't it?

Don't tell Lou, honey, but if Dot moves to D.C., I'll be one surprised person – but not the only one. If I understand these people correctly, I think she's nuts – how about you? I love you and miss you terrifically – Be sweet and hurry after your family. Bye for now.

Love you – your own,

Mommy

February 20, 1945 – from Ann in Poughkeepsie, NY

Monday
Feb. 19, 1945

Hello skunk,

What's the matter – having too much fun with that red-head? Here I write every nite and not a word – not even a card from my supposed lover. What goes on here?

If you don't write soon I'm going to crack up. Helluva way to treat a pregnant woman! I must say!

Am looking forward to the weekend. Went shopping today with Dot. We took Dougie and Carol. They were pretty good, but boy am I dead! So is Dot. They're both sawing logs all to pieces and its just 5 of 8 now! I could really be doing the same right now!

So Lou spent Sat nite with you. What else did you do. Darn, the only way I hear of you is in the letter Dot received every morning!

You'd better bring me a peace pipe when you come or there's going to be a Cajun on a Texan and not the way you're planning either! Hmmm..., looks like I got into Carol's stationery!

Well, sweet, I'm going up, take a bath, and put the two of us to bed. Am worn out after the excursion into town. Enjoyed Sunday very much. Dot's sister, husband and little boy had dinner with us. Then we all went over to Aunt Jenny's for supper and Uncle Tom showed me his fishing tackle. Honey, that's sompin! I know you'd enjoy his collection. Worth hundreds I'll bet.

Take it easy and try picking up a pen – it's not hard at all. See I told you!

Good nite, sweet sleep tite!

I love you all my life.

Your Baby

Feb. 22, 1945 – This letter is from Bill, Special Delivery from Washington D.C., To Ann in Poughkeepsie, NY. Bill's letter is written on an envelope from a letter that someone wrote to Bill, from 2405 Albans Road, Houston, TX.

Feb. 22 Thursday

My dear loving wife and baby,

Well here I go again writing on my fancy stationary. Hope you don't mind. But it does give it that Abe Lincoln touch, you know. The weather is simply lovely here this morn. That good old Calif kind – real nice and juicy – I bet it's cold up there. Been receiving your letters right along and am really getting lonesome for you all. In fact, you can't imagine how I have missed you these past 2 weeks. Am leaving here Sat about noon but Lou won't come with me. He is leaving Friday. The Capt doesn't want both of us gone too long at the same time. I have to be back in MDW by 5:00pm Tuesday.

There is really not much new around here – more or less the same old 6 & 7. The Founea's have really been swell. They ask me to supper most every nite. Played Monopoly with them and Bob and Statia last nite. We got our coal Monday. I am at the post office again writing this. Looks as though that is the only time I will write – on the way home from work. If I wait until I get home, I say I'll write when I wake up and when I wake up I go to Andre's and Rita's and eat and before I know if it is time to go to work again. I'm really a hell of a sort of guy aren't I, Mommy, but you love me don't you. I love you too. I'll let you all know when I arrive at the station in Poughkeepsie. Will call you from station. Lou said you and Dot and he would meet me. I'm enclosing couple of letters and now I had better close and go home and go to bed.

ILUAML

Popsie

P.S.: Kiss Carol for me and tell all hello.

Note: ILUAML means "I love you all my life"

This last letter is from Ann, however, it wasn't accompanied by an envelope, so I'm not sure exactly when it was written. I will include it here at the end, just so it's included, even though it is not included chronologically. Based on the content of the letter, I believe this was written while Ann and Carol were staying at her parents' Missouri Ave. house, and I believe it was written in mid-March 1944. However, it's almost as if Ann, or God, set this particular letter aside so that it could be the last in this compilation.

Monday

Hi Honey,

Just received the card you sent and it was so welcome. Both the baby and I wanted to eat it up. She

Carol, Bill, Ann, and new baby William Robert, Washington D.C., c. 1945.

just woke up and she's pushing the little cart around the room. It's early to start your letter but I just felt like I wanted to talk to my O.A.O. The baby keeps hunting for you. She woke up this morning calling you and pointing down the stairs, wanting to go down right away to see you. She just knew you were down there. She's walked into everyone's heart around here and Aunt Tennie comes in in the evening calling her and she just runs. I went over to the drug store and they said the pictures should be there tomorrow or Wed. I hope you have barracks by then. I'll send Max's letter, too, and by the way, the Cummins have a 7 ½ lb. baby boy, born March 5 and he's Thomas Leo Cummins III. I know they must be proud. You remember how they acted around Carol – I can just imagine how they're carrying on with one of their own.

I wrote Mom and Pop this morning and mailed it. I told them not to send anything, just write to you to that address. I imagine you sent a card to them too, but I didn't know about that this morning. I hope you call again soon. This time I promise not to be so taken aback and will be able to talk sense. I guess you really saw Texas, eh? Gosh, that really must make you feel important – dashing you all over the country to outwit spies – my, but you're important!

I just talked to Dorothy and Van goes down for his final physical and Dorothy is worried, but she said that his boss told him he had a six month deferment approved by the state board, however it has to be approved by the local board after he's been examined to find whether he's passed or not. I'm going to call Lila Lee Hall tonight to find out about R. Do you know anything about him? Oh yes, while we are still thinking of Van – their address is 2517 Huldy, Hou 6, Tex. Any other addresses I've forgotten?

Well, sweet, I'm going to have to close for now. I have to go to the store so will write more later. Maybe I can think of something a little more interesting to tell my guy. So long 'til later...

Just finished my nightly chores of putting our little bebe to bye bye land. She was ready, as usual –

I put the ration of books and your gas books in an envelope with a letter tell – the why – for and will give it to Aunt Tennie to mail with this in the morning. I know I must keep those tire inspection papers and car papers and gas coupons in a safe place, but I also must carry them in my purse so I confiscated your new billfold. I feel awfully guilty about it, so if you want it, I'll bring it when we see you and you can let me have your old one. I hate to hurt Sis and I'm sure if you don't say you want it, she will be. She paid for it out of her first paycheck and I know you must value it a lot. I know I do. I must have one, though, so I'll use yours – OK? OK!

Listen, sweet, as long as I'm on the "must-have" list, I know one thing I can do without no longer – a picture of my lover – so please, won't you have one, a large one, made for my dresser and a small one made for my wallet? You'll have some snaps of your two girls before the week is out but your two girls haven't anything to look at except the picture we hold in our hearts. Of course, that's enough at night in bed but during the day, it's kind of hard to take out your heart and have a look at it during the daytime – please?

Sweet, where did you say those bank-deposit envelopes were? And did you get the statement and, if so, where is it? I want to check my checkbook and get straight on our balance. When the IBM checks start coming through, I'm marching myself down to the bank so I can put it in the savings account. Then I'll mail the G.I. checks to the drawing account. Is that right? I seem to be a bit foggy on some things and just wanted to check with you on this. Every once in a while, I'll remember something I wanted to ask you and I think of C42705 and have to check myself. Then I want to cry – but I don't! Haven't since last Thursday evening. (Proud of me?)

Golly, I hope to goodness I have a letter from His Nibs to help me get through another day. Tomorrow, Aunt Tennie and I are going to Sears to get some chocolates to save for us to eat on Sundays. I've given that up for Lent and something else too, but if I were to be with you before but was over, I'm sure I'd break that one.

I really must go now. It isn't polite to sit up here and write hour upon hour, so I guess I'd better end this epistle and give out with a little conversation to the ladies – and then, to bed, to dream of that guy! I wonder who he could be? Can you guess? I betcha can!

Will write more tomorrow night so until then, sweetheart, I'll always remain.

All yours –

Baby Anne

P.S.: Good Nite, sweet, sleep tight – I love you all my life.

Above right: Bill and Baby Ann on an Alaskan cruise in the mid 1990's. Below right: Bill visiting (with Baby Ann as photographer) the World War II Memorial in Washington, D.C., c. 2006. Bill was stationed in Washington D.C. during his war service, working in the quarter-master general's office in the War Department.

~ April 12, 1940 ~

You are cordially invited to the
70th Wedding Anniversary
Celebration for

Bill and Ann Genzer

Made in the USA
Lexington, KY
25 February 2014